Language Guides

Developing Handwriting

Editor: Dr Joyce M. Morris

Language Guides

Developing Handwriting

Peter Smith

Primary Adviser, Greater London
Borough of Hillingdon

Macmillan Education

First published 1977
Reprinted 1978, 1979

Published by
MACMILLAN EDUCATION LTD
London and Basingstoke
Associated companies and representatives
throughout the world

Printed in Hong Kong by
Wing King Tong Co Ltd

Set in Monotype Plantin

Contents

ACKNOWLEDGEMENTS vi

INTRODUCTION vii

AUTHOR'S VIEWPOINT ix

1 Historical perspective 1

2 Preparing children to learn print-script 6

3 Print-script 12

4 Joined handwriting: choosing the style 26

5 Teaching joined writing 39

6 Maintaining and improving standards of handwriting 52

7 Diagnosis and eradication of faults 59

FINAL WORD 76

AIDS FOR TEACHING HANDWRITING 78

ADDRESSES 80

BIBLIOGRAPHY 81

INDEX 93

Acknowledgements

I should like to thank those teachers in Inner London and Hillingdon who I have observed teaching handwriting at various stages or who have discussed their techniques and problems with me. In particular, I should like to express my thanks to Margaret MacIntyre, headmistress of Sulivan Primary School in Fulham from 1951 to 1971. Miss MacIntyre was an exceptional teacher and, before the Second World War, she assisted Marion Richardson in the development of her handwriting scheme. I am greatly indebted to Margaret for all she taught me during the years I was her deputy.

The author and publishers also wish to thank the following for permission to include examples and/or extracts from their publications: Margaret Newton of the University of Aston, Lyn Wendon of Pictograms, Autobates Learning Systems Ltd, Ginn & Co. Ltd, Thomas Nelson and Sons Ltd, Osmiroid Ltd, Platignum Ltd, and the University of London Press.

Introduction

Over the years, the growth of a reverential attitude towards children's creativity has tended to obscure the important role of handwriting in their written expression and in the acquisition of literacy generally. This, in turn, has led to a frequent complaint that handwriting is neglected in today's schools; a complaint, alas, not without substance according to survey findings in the Bullock Report.

Be that as it may, no such charge could be made against the large urban school of which Peter Smith was headmaster before becoming a Primary Adviser. Certainly, under his leadership, it exemplified the modern emphasis on children learning rather than subject teaching. At the same time, through the provision of curriculum guidelines and regular staff meetings to discuss them, teachers were encouraged to follow an agreed school policy of sound instruction and ample practice for the development of handwriting as for all other basic skills.

Essentially, this language guide is a more detailed version of the handwriting guideline which the author prepared for his own school staff. It begins with his views on educational issues of current concern to show, amongst other things, that a child-centred philosophy of education is not incompatible with a traditional concern for the 'second R'. More-over, handwriting is recognised as an art form as well as a skill to be cultivated, not, as is often supposed, by mechanical drill and the dull copying of material devoid of other value.

With prevalent misunderstandings out of the way, the author sets his subject in historical perspective with just enough detail to highlight the possibilities of handwriting as a fruitful topic for study by primary school pupils. He then devotes the rest of his discussion to all that is involved in ensuring that they eventually develop a running hand which, in the words of the Bullock Report is 'simultaneously legible, fast-flowing, and individual and becomes effortless to produce'.

As an essential first step towards achieving that objective, this illustrated text is designed to help teachers decide an effective school programme. It makes clear what is available to them and their pupils in terms of writing styles, classroom materials, methods of instruction and practice. It also acknowledges their right to choose freely from the alternatives presented, whilst leaving no doubt about the author's preferences for print-script at the infant stage, followed by the Marion Richardson style for lower-juniors and a modified form of Italic handwriting thereafter. In other words, description precedes prescription, and acceptance or rejection of what is advocated is left to the professional judgement of teachers. Likewise, controversial issues are presented in a manner which leaves the reader to decide whether the author has made a good case for such practices as teaching infants to cope with both upper and lower-case letters from the very beginning.

However, although Peter Smith emphasises the positive role and responsibilities of today's teachers, he is obviously sympathetic to them and the problems they have to face. For instance, at the risk of being considered reactionary, he provides reassurance from his own wealth of experience that large group instruction is not only an economical technique, but it is sometimes more desirable than individual instruction. He also describes in a down-to-earth fashion how to eradicate writing faults, and suggests effective strategies for dealing with the special problems of slow learners and other minority groups in ordinary school circumstances.

Not surprisingly, the main substance of *Developing Handwriting* has already been used to good effect on in-service courses. In consequence, there is reason to believe that this rich source of detailed practical guidance will be welcomed by teachers everywhere, not least because it amplifies what the Bullock Report has to say about the same important subject.

August 1976   JOYCE M. MORRIS

Author's viewpoint

There seems to be considerable confusion about the role of the primary-school teacher in the nineteen-seventies. Advocates of 'progressive', child-centred approaches to education have properly emphasised the importance of activity, involvement, motivation, creativity, the rich classroom environment, and so on. However, because these approaches are partly a reaction to formal class teaching, there is a tendency to neglect the role of the teacher as instructor.

Although I fully agree with the emphasis being placed on children learning rather than on subject teaching, there are areas of the basic skills which can only be mastered through well-organised instruction. It is also important that this instruction is offered at the right time for each child, neither too soon nor too late. Skills lessons given before children appreciate the need for them, and before they are ready, can and do cause them confusion and anxiety. On the other hand, to delay teaching relevant basic skills leads to boredom and frustration.

If teachers are to make such critical judgements and to succeed in the very diverse roles they have to play in the modern primary school, they must be well prepared and informed. For instance, they require knowledge of alternative learning theories, of child development, of the various possibilities of school and classroom organisation, and of the wide range of materials and equipment available. They must also be thoroughly versed in the content of the primary-school curriculum. Furthermore, they must understand the academic disciplines of the subjects to be taught and be aware of the sequence in which some basic skills are acquired.

The need for training and guidance

These requirements make a formidable list, and may ask too much of many teachers unless leadership, guidance and continuing in-service training is made available to them. Accordingly, it is a heartening sign that one of the most widely accepted recommendations in the James Report (6) is the proposal to establish a comprehensive programme of in-service training in the 'third cycle'.

The significance of this change is that the first cycle of further education consists of two years of broadly-based studies leading to the diploma in higher education, and obviating the necessity for premature commitment to the teaching profession. The second cycle would be devoted to one year of pre-service training for teaching, whilst the third cycle is envisaged as a highly-structured and supportive induction year.

The DES White Paper, *Education: a Framework for Expansion* (5), gives teeth to this recommendation. It proposed a substantial expansion of in-service training in 1974–75, followed by progressively increasing provision to reach a target of three per cent release by 1981. Achieving this target would make possible a long-awaited sabbatical term for all teachers.

Given adequate help and support and, most important, time to grow so that they are able to work comfortably and efficiently at each stage of their development as teachers, at least there is hope of approaching the ideal so many seek. There would also be fewer teachers feeling inadequate in chaotic non-learning situations into which they stumble through lack of professional understanding.

Nevertheless I have misgivings about the first and second cycles of teacher training as recommended by the James Report (6). It seems an unfortunate contradiction that, at the same time as proposing welcome improvements in provision for in-service training, the James Committee proposed a drastic reduction in the initial professional preparation of teachers. I fear that, if and when the James proposals are fully implemented, the teacher-tutors, on whose abilities the quality of the probationary year will so much depend, will find that probationers have even greater gaps in their professional training than at present.

The skills of handwriting do not appear to have figured very largely in the three-year courses of recent years. Thus ways must be found of convincing all concerned of the importance of dealing with this key topic adequately in the future, despite a possible reduction in the total time available.

As a head-teacher, I tried to meet the need for guidance through day-to-day contacts with my colleagues, staff meetings, and the provision of a written series of guidelines. As a lecturer in language arts for in-service training courses I am very much aware that a considerable proportion of teachers feel unsure about what they are doing in the classroom and feel they lack knowledge of the nature of language and of teaching techniques for helping children to acquire the basic literacy skills.

One very common misunderstanding is that any instruction a teacher provides must be given to children individually. Some young teachers have been made to feel guilty if they fall short of this ideal by giving a lesson to a group. But surely we must accept that great skill, experience and dedication are needed for a teacher to be able to give adequate individual attention to every child in a class of thirty-five or more. Anyway, it is doubtful whether a total emphasis on individual instruction is in the interests of the children. After all, there is much value in the interaction between members of a group as they endeavour to come to grips with a problem. Indeed, the most economic use of a teacher's time in developing basic skills in children would seem to be through group work, for which children are grouped according to their needs, at least during part of the day. At other times they may be working individually or in groups developing interests or creative themes. The diagram below clarifies this principle.

CLASS ORGANISATION

		Individuals	Groups	Whole Class
	Free			
METHOD OF WORKING	Under Control			
	Under Direction			

In the above diagram the term 'free' does not mean that children are at liberty to do what they like without consideration for others, or that they should be free to do nothing at all. Nevertheless, in a well-organised classroom, with materials readily available, good pupil–teacher relationships, and a lively curriculum, it is possible to allow considerable choice and freedom for children to pursue their own interests within prescribed limits. Moreover, it has been my experience that opportunities of this nature are not abused by children, and the work produced at such times is usually high in quality.

The term 'under control' is used to describe those situations in which children have some degree of choice with regard to content and/or materials, but in which they are subject to limitations imposed by group aims. For example, a child preparing a report on one aspect of a group topic may have been (a) involved in the choice of topic, (b) allowed to select a particular aspect for study, and (c) permitted freedom in deciding what materials to use. At the same time there will be an obligation to keep to the agreed brief and to meet a particular deadline.

The third heading 'under direction' covers those occasions when the teacher determines that because of the nature of the learning task and the needs of the child it is necessary to direct the work of the child more formally. In other words, the teacher assumes, for a time, the didactic role of instructor.

The three horizontal headings and three vertical headings give rise to nine different categories. I would suggest that in any given class, some of the work being done would fit into each of those categories over a period of, say, a fortnight.

Bearing all this in mind, a consideration of handwriting naturally underlines the fact that it is an educational technique; the normal vehicle for the creative art of written expression. It can also be thought of as an art form and there is no doubt that well-formed, attractive handwriting can be a pleasure to the beholder as well as a great source of joy and pride for the writer. As teachers, we have to adopt a sensible position and help our children achieve a pleasant, quick, fluent style of handwriting and, except perhaps for display purposes, avoid over-emphasising the aesthetic quality of writing to the detriment of the content of the written expression.

Clearly it is very important to provide efficient teaching and adequate practice of handwriting skills. Indeed these necessities are highlighted by Sybil Marshall in her recent book *Creative Writing* (24). Though well known for her encouragement of creative approaches, she devotes several pages to the acquisition of handwriting skills. For example, she writes:

> My purpose is to make a plea for recognition that this [skill in handwriting] is a prerequisite for any successful attempt at creative writing.

The vast majority of children need a systematic course of instruction if they are to learn to form the letters of the alphabet properly. Even the minority of very able children who seem to be able to work out the sound–symbol relationships of the English language with minimal help are likely to form the letters incorrectly without guidance. My aim in this guide will be to suggest ways in which the skills of handwriting can be efficiently taught to primary-age children, whether they are learning in a child-centred classroom or a more formally organised one.

Further Reading

Blackie, J. (1)
The former H.M. Chief Inspector of Primary Schools begins Chapter 9 of his book, *Changing the Primary School*, with a most interesting expression of his views on handwriting in the primary school.

Department of Education and Science (5)

Department of Education and Science (6)
The James Report on the future training of teachers.

Jarman, C. (21)
A short article in which the whole problem of teaching handwriting is discussed.

Marshall, S. (24)
The essential need for systematic teaching of handwriting skills as a prerequisite for success in creative writing is discussed (pp. 19–24).

Moyle, D. (26)
There is a discussion of the place of formal learning in the informal infants' school (pp. 99–102).

Taylor, J. (34)
Interspersed with other aspects of a sequential development of literacy skills is a discussion of the teacher's role in developing handwriting skills (pp. 86–92, 117, 119–20, 151–2 and 165).

Yardley, A. (40)
Describes the teacher's role in developing handwriting skills in Chapter 18 on imaginative writing.

1

Historical perspective

It is interesting to consider the ways in which systems of writing gradually evolved as civilisation progressed. A recent book by Alfred Fairbank (8) describes and illustrates this evolution fully. From his book, and others listed in the bibliography, the history of handwriting and the social effects of different kinds of writing may be studied in detail. The purpose of this chapter is simply to summarise the main trends.

The ability to write seemed so remarkable to ancient peoples that they attributed magical or religious qualities to those who possessed the skill. The early Egyptians believed that the gods Thoth and Isis gave them the knowledge of writing, while the Babylonians gave credit to Nebo, the Greeks to Hermes and the Hindus to Brahma. Moreover, the father of Chinese writing, Ts'ang Chieh, was thought to be so perceptive that he had been endowed with an extra pair of eyes.

Research and discoveries, particularly in the caves of Spain and France, have revealed that the beginning of recorded communication was in the form of pictures painted on the walls of caves. These pictures may sometimes have been painted to satisfy an artistic urge but it is thought there was often a purpose to them. Perhaps they played a part in the celebration of fertility rites or in the pursuit of a hunted beast, or they may have been a reminder of a momentous event. From these first pictures early man developed picture writing which he may have used as an aid to memory or as a record of a transaction. These pictograms were simple drawings of a significant part of an object and were used to represent the whole.

The first people in history to develop a full system of written language were the Sumerians who, by about the year 2500 BC, were using a monosyllabic system developed from simple pictograms and ideograms. The change from curved to straight lines resulted from the use of a triangular-shaped reed as the stylus. The mark produced on a clay tablet by a wedge-shaped stylus is naturally a straight line and this is an early example of the way in which the available materials may influence the style of writing of the time. This wedge-shaped writing was called 'cuneiform' from the Latin *cuneus* meaning wedge.

The Ancient Egyptians used three different scripts. From about the year 3000 BC until the time of Christ, they used the 'hieroglyphic' style which changed very little through this long period of time. Hieroglyphics were mainly used for inscriptions on buildings and monuments and consisted of simplified formalised pictures in vertical columns carved on stone. However, out of this evolved the 'hieratic' style which developed because of two particular circumstances: the invention of papyrus made it possible to write with brush or reed pen and thus more speedily and with less restriction; and fluency was further increased by the change from writing vertically to writing horizontally – from right to left at this time. The third style of writing used by the Ancient Egyptians first appeared about the year 700 BC and was called 'demotic'. It was a rapid, fluent, cursive style and was a departure from the pictorial quality of hieroglyphics.

The written languages of modern Western civilisations are, of course, based on a collection of symbols called letters which are written to represent the sounds used in speech. However unsatisfactory our present alphabet may be, there can be no doubt whatever that the development of civilisation as we know it today owes much to the invention of the alphabet. We shall probably never know who invented the very first alphabet nor precisely when, but historians do suggest that Byblos was the place where it may all have begun. Certainly the inscription on the sarcophagus of King Ahiram of Byblos used an alphabet of twenty-two letters and is believed to have been carved in the eleventh century BC. From the Semitic alphabet of Byblos developed the Phoenician alphabet, which was also influenced by Egyptian writing. There were still only twenty-two letters, none of which was a vowel. The first two letters were named 'aleph' and 'beth'. Then the Greeks adapted the Phoenician alphabet by adding vowels. They called the first two letters 'alpha' and 'beta' and it is from these two names that the word 'alphabet' was derived. The Greeks also changed the direction of their horizontal writing so that it was written from left to right, a far more natural direction for a right-handed person. There was an interesting intermediary stage when writing was in opposite directions on alternate lines in ploughman style. The correct term for that confusing practice is 'boustrophedon'.

The alphabet we use today follows very closely the one which the Romans developed in the centuries immediately preceding the birth of Christ. It was based on the framework acquired from the Greeks and has never been surpassed for its beauty. The capital letters forming the inscription at the base of the Trajan column in Rome are excellent examples of the proportion and grace of the Roman alphabet and serve as the model for our present-day printing type. The letters of the inscription have the characteristic 'thicks' and 'thins' because, although they were cut with a chisel and mallet, they were first set out with a broad brush.

The Roman alphabet consisted of only capital letters which, as they were used for the handwriting of books, tended to become more rounded because a pen on parchment makes curved strokes more easily than straight ones. By the sixth century AD scribes had evolved an alphabet of half-uncials. These are generally known as the 'small' letters but are better called the 'lower-case' letters since any symbol may be written large or small in size. The term 'lower-case' is derived from the practice of arranging the compositor's type in two sets of cases. The less-used capital letters are kept in the upper cases while the more frequently needed 'small' letters are stored in the lower cases.

The pen used for writing was the goose quill (the name 'pen' deriving from *penna* which is Latin for feather). The quill was cut by the scribe himself and was given a broad tip for longer wear. Such a nib gives rise to the characteristic thick and thin strokes without need for variation in pressure. It also became accepted that writing with the pen held at an angle of forty-five degrees to the line of writing enabled the scribe to write faster and to fit more words on to a line.

As well as the formal scripts used in the writing of books there were cursive scripts also based on the half-uncials, which developed in the course of the informal writing used in correspondence and in personal note-taking. The first 'Italic' hand is thought to have been invented by a Florentine scholar called Niccole Niccoli who made use of diagonal joins and up-strokes as he wrote at speed avoiding pen-lifts. He also altered the shapes of some letters and changed proportions of others.

The introduction of printing presses for the mass production of books had a considerable impact on the development of hand-writing styles. This was not so marked at first when wood blocks were the medium for printing. Scribes wrote on transparent paper which was then stuck face down on the wood block. Thus a mirror image of the writing was provided and master engravers cut away the surrounding area leaving the raised letters to be inked for printing. The change came when longer-lasting metal plates were favoured instead of wood blocks. These copper plates were engraved with an instrument called a 'burin' which cuts a fine line when used lightly and a wider and deeper groove as greater pressure is applied. This different technique resulted in the invention of the Copperplate style of writing characterised by loops to ascenders and descenders. The loops were designed to permit the writing of whole words without lifting the pen.

When Copperplate writing is executed on paper with pen and ink, the only suitable nib is a pointed, flexible one with which 'thicks' and 'thins' are made by varying pressure to change the extent to which the split top parts of the nib spread. The monitors in the Joseph Lancaster Schools in the nineteenth century must have warmly welcomed the arrival of flexible steel pen-nibs which relieved them of the laborious daily task of cutting new pointed tips to their scholars' quills.

This short introduction to the fascinating history of the development of handwriting brings us up to the time of compulsory education for all in Britain. In 1870 the basis of elementary education was instruction in the three Rs – reading, writing and arithmetic. Writing in those days meant the mechanical skills of handwriting and though, happily, the emphasis has now changed to the expressive aspects of the skill, we must still ensure that the mechanical skills are well taught. Without them written expression is not possible and the children are frustrated in their attempts to communicate.

The history of man's progress in developing the art of written communication is a very fruitful topic for junior children to study. It is hoped that this brief outline, perhaps supplemented by the books recommended below, may be helpful in this connexion.

Further Reading

Fairbanks, A. (8)
The Story of Handwriting provides a comprehensive history of the origins and development of handwriting with copious illustrations. There is also a bibliography with many suggestions for further reading for those who wish to pursue the topic.

Gourdie, T. (11)
The development of modern handwriting from Egyptian times to the present is briefly surveyed in the first few pages.

Whanslaw, H. W. (39)
A brief illustrated history of the development of writing and printing, together with a short account of the compilation, translation and distribution of the Bible.

2

Preparing children to learn print-script

When children start school some will already be able to write and others will be ready to learn. However, many new entrants will not be so ready and the teacher must observe them at their varied activities in order to judge when each child reaches the stage of development at which there is a reasonable chance of experiencing success in learning to write.

It is not suggested that the teacher should watch and wait for this moment of readiness without making provision to help bring it about. Research has shown that reading readiness is not dependent solely on maturation but can be affected by training. This applies equally to readiness for writing. A thoughtful teacher, therefore, in the range of provision in her classroom, will include many activities and experiences designed to foster the development of motivation, motor skills, visual perception and memory recall.

Motivation

It is of paramount importance that children are motivated to write by helping them to see the purpose and nature of written language. (Detailed suggestions for this are given in Chapter 4.) Indeed without their having this understanding and an interest in and love of books, any attempt to introduce children to the mysteries of our written symbols is likely to be fruitless.

Motor Skills

Because any attempt to write involves the controlled use of fine muscles, activities designed to give practice in using these muscles are desirable. An imaginative teacher will be able to think of numerous suitable activities in addition to the following suggestions:

a) Three-dimensional modelling with plastic materials, such as clay, plasticine, dough, and with cardboard boxes and other 'junk' materials

b) Work with chalk on the wall-board or individual small boards; an economical activity because it is easy to erase

c) Drawing in sand with a finger or stick; also easily erased with a sand rake

d) Model-making with large plastic Meccano and other suitable constructional toys

e) Building bricks, blocks and mechanical toys

f) Cutting out material or paper with scissors

g) Tracing simple outline pictures as a preliminary to tracing own name and other familiar words

h) Drawing with templates and colouring the outline shapes produced

i) Joining together dots to form a picture

j) Picture and pattern making with finger paints, brush paints, crayons and jumbo pencils (this kind of art work is increasingly done vertically on easels and it is important to ensure that horizontal surfaces are also used, since the position of hands in relation to the body is so different). The use of felt pens is also recommended.

Children should be introduced to patterns based on basic writing shapes. These patterns, when drawn fluently and continuously from left to right, aid the development of the muscular control required to form the different letters, as well as reinforcing left-to-right orientation. At this stage they should be drawn boldly – perhaps two inches high, and the children should be encouraged to colour in the shapes, such as those below, with crayon or paint. The children enjoy making writing patterns and experience great pleasure when they learn to draw lines of pattern consecutively and are encouraged to explore the background patterns thus created.

Practice should also be provided in making patterns from straight lines, vertical, horizontal and diagonal, since these form the basis of the majority of capital letters.

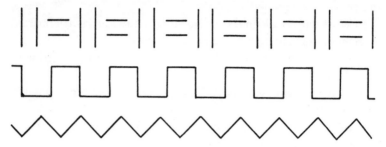

The fundamental importance of writing patterns for the development of motor skills and as the basis for all future writing is widely recognised, and most manuals on handwriting include recommendations and advice about them. However, it is in the Marion Richardson scheme that the fullest attention to pattern work may be found and an examination of the *Writing and Writing Patterns* Teacher's Book (30) will prove most valuable.

The Teacher's Manual for the reading scheme *Time for Reading* (28) also includes a most helpful appendix on writing patterns in which much practical advice on developing pattern-making with young children is offered. The connexion between patterns and later writing is mentioned and the point is made that letter 'c' presents the greatest difficulty of motor control. The authors suggest that since letters 'a', 'd', 'g' and 'q' are based on letter 'c', it is rewarding to devote considerable time to this letter pattern.

Basic Motor Skills (17) is a series of eight workbooks, providing a highly structured scheme to aid the development of pre-writing motor skills. The authors, Simon Haskell and Margaret Paull, have devised a series of finely-graded exercises, progressing from drawing a straight line along a wide road, through more complicated shapes, to the eventual formation of single letters of the alphabet.

At this point it should be stressed that some of the above suggestions are offered as appropriate to the needs of only the minority of children whose motor-skill development is retarded. In no sense is the pursuit of these highly-structured activities advocated as a substitute for the creative work which is to be found in a good infants' school.

Visual perception

The shapes of the alphabet letters differ in varying degree, the difference in form sometimes being very slight indeed. In some cases the difference is one of inversion or reversal, so children must be helped to appreciate that there is a 'right' angle from which to view table games and puzzles. Inset picture puzzles which have people and objects facing in different directions can help introduce small children to ideas of orientation. A teacher must give thought to the arrangement of furniture in the classroom in this respect. The practice of grouping tables together could result in children playing matching games, and games of the word 'lotto' type, with an upside-down view of their opponents' cards.

However, if children lack the ability to discriminate between two fairly similar symbols, there would appear to be little prospect of their being capable of learning to make various letters correctly. The teachers' manuals for most modern reading schemes contain advice and suggestions for apparatus and exercises to improve powers of visual discrimination, and such work should also aid in the preparation for learning to write. Manufacturers of teaching materials often include items in their catalogues which are useful in this direction. Furthermore, infant teachers are renowned for their ingenuity in devising apparatus to meet the needs of their children. The following suggestions are offered as examples of appropriate materials (some of which are available from manufacturers) which give young children experience of the two-dimensional nature of symbols:

a) Jigsaw puzzles (visual discrimination is entailed in selecting pieces that fit together)

b) Matching games based on snap cards or dominoes, including picture dominoes

c) Classification of geometric shapes and other sorting materials

d) Reproduction of shapes by drawing or modelling

e) Matching pictures related to the reading scheme

f) Matching written language by pairing identical sentence or word flash-cards; flash-cards repeating the living language round the room can be matched with captions

g) Recognising the 'odd one out' in a series of otherwise identical drawings. This kind of puzzle is popular in children's comics.

Teachers can devise simplified versions based on simple drawings, symbols, letters or words; exercises can also be duplicated or produced in the form of work-cards

h) Commercially-produced attribute blocks can be used for games in which children classify colour, shape, size or thickness

i) The popular party game of remembering and describing the object which has been removed from a group of objects concentrates attention on the visual

j) Identification of nature specimens by comparison with clear photographs or simple accurate drawings

k) Finding hidden objects in pictures

l) The second wave of *Language in Action*, levels 0 and 0-1, (25), deals specifically with problems of visual perception.

In all of these activities it is essential for teachers to draw attention to details and differences and to provide the language alongside the activity.

Memory recall

For a child to experience progression in learning to write he must retain his previous learning. Thus a child who has learned the sound, shape and correct way to form a letter should later be able to recall and reproduce the letter at will. It follows that games and activities which improve visual memory are an essential part of the preparation for learning to write for many children. Useful ideas in this connexion include:

a) The reproduction of a simplified outline drawing after a brief exposure of the original

b) The reproduction of a sequence of simple pictures or symbols

c) The reproduction of a sequence of various numbers of dots

d) The reproduction of a sequence of colours

e) Completion of drawings of common objects which have certain parts missing

f) The reproduction of a letter shape learned previously.

Learning Development Aids have recently produced a set of visual recall cards which are suitable for training in memory recall of visual patterns. The use of these cards in a one-to-one situation also gives rise to useful discussion. (See list of Aids for Teaching Handwriting, pages 78-9.)

Slow learners

Inevitably some children progress towards literacy much slower than the majority. Such children may be helped by continued and increased provision of the kind of activities discussed in this chapter, together with as much individual attention as can be given. Many of the slow starters will respond to extra help and time. But specific suggestions are needed for helping children who continue to experience difficulty, and these are given in Chapter 7.

Of course teachers of slow-learning pupils need to familiarise themselves with the children's backgrounds and seek clues there as to possible causes of learning difficulties. They should also discuss the problems of such children with their head-teacher and, if necessary, consult the school doctor and educational psychologist.

Further Reading

Brennan, W. *et al.* (2)
The Teacher's Handbook for the *Look* series discusses the various sub-skills required for handwriting and other literacy skills. The four workbooks provide appropriate exercises for the children and extend the suggestions made in this guide.

Haskell, S. and Paull, M. (17)
A description of the workbook series, *Basic Motor Skills Booklets*, together with a discussion of the underlying theories.

Morris, J. M. *et al.* (25)

Obrist, C. and Pickard, P. (28)
Helpful advice and practical suggestions for the development of writing patterns are offered in Appendix B.

Richardson, M. (30)

Stern, C. and Gould, T. S. (32)
An approach to aid memory recall of letter shapes is discussed.

Smith, P. and Williams, J. (43)
Writemaster Book 1. A book of 32 Pressure-fax spiritmasters providing activities to foster the skills and attitudes discussed in this chapter. Notes of guidance for children and teachers are included. Books 2 and 3 deal with the learning and practice of print-script.

3

Print-script

Print-script is the style of handwriting most commonly taught in the first two or three years of schooling. It was introduced in London schools during the First World War despite vigorous opposition to its adoption. It proved to be so successful that the international survey of reading and writing carried out for UNESCO by William S. Gray (14) advocated its general adoption throughout the western world. The main advantages of print-script over cursive styles, during the early years, are generally held to be:

a) the letters have simpler forms

b) the alphabet is the same as the children meet in reading and so confusion is avoided

c) print-script is similar to drawing

d) no strokes are needed for joining

e) children using print-script are able to express their ideas on paper more quickly

f) there are fewer failures

g) print-script allows comparison with printed letters

h) there is less eye-strain than with cursive writing

i) the rounded shapes of the letters are more suited to the muscular and motor development of small children than the elliptical ones associated with most joined styles.

Critics of print-script claim that, at the time of transition to joined writing, the child has to learn a new set of letter shapes. This is an exaggeration. Providing that print-script has been well taught, the only major change, apart from the addition of ligatures, is the transition from round to elliptical shape and from upright to slanting strokes. If this transition is made at the right stage of physical development it is a fairly easy one.

However, it is essential to guard against incorrect or inadequate teaching of letter formation and the simplification of print-script into 'ball and stick' is to be strongly deprecated. 'Ball and stick' is a method of teaching print-script which suggests that all letters are composed of separate curved or straight lines. Thus letter 'a' is formed from a ball and a short stick and letter 'd' from a circle and a longer stick. Teaching this method of making letters establishes bad habits that will take a great deal of time and effort to break at a later stage. Indeed, many teachers are worried that their young pupils, if left to find their own way of forming letters, may develop habits that will be a handicap to the later acquisition of a well-formed running hand.

This misgiving calls into question the whole concept of the teacher's role in the nineteen-seventies. While most teachers want their children to learn actively and purposefully, pursuing their individual interests, interacting with a rich classroom environment and enjoying opportunities to be creative in a variety of media, there are many who are concerned about how to provide the instruction and guidance in skills and processes that are essential for the children's continuing progress. Whether the approach to learning is highly innovatory or more formally oriented, provision must be made for teaching the correct methods of forming letters. The children may be taught individually or in groups, depending on the stages of development of the children concerned, the skill of the teacher and which approach the teacher feels comfortable in using.

Capital and lower-case letters

There is considerable controversy over the order of teaching capital letters and lower-case letters at the early stages of acquiring literacy skills. For a long time teachers have despaired at the number of children who start school in the reception classes happily making capital letters but having no knowledge of the lower-case forms. This has led to confusion on meeting the predominantly lower-case letters in reading primers, and to indiscriminate use of capitals in children's first attempts at writing. Indeed many teachers have asked parents of pre-school children to leave the whole business of teaching reading and writing to the school.

There is a current theory, and some experts are numbered

among its supporters, which advocates initial learning of reading and writing through capitals only. This proposition is advanced because capital letters are both more easily formed and more readily differentiated. The adoption of this recommendation would, however, necessitate the production of early reading matter in capitals only and would exclude children from traditional print in the early stages.

On the other hand, some experts, including the authors of *Breakthrough to Literacy* (23), prefer to concentrate on lower-case letters only in the early stages and to ignore the existence of capitals till later. Consequently, the first twelve books for children in the *Breakthrough* series are printed without any capitals. Even this deliberate policy is not entirely satisfactory as it cannot shield children from exposure to capital letters in their home and neighbourhood environments.

Although it means a double learning load in terms of shape recognition, I feel that children must learn to cope with both forms of letters from the beginning, with priority being given to the lower-case shapes since they will be more frequently used in both reading and writing at all stages.

It is also important for teachers to encourage parents of preschool children to foster an early start with spoken language and other fundamental pre-literacy skills. In this connexion, parents need to be made consciously aware of the relatively greater importance of lower-case letters in writing. It is helpful to prepare a leaflet for parents, giving them some guidelines, which can be handed to them when their children are enrolled. A useful example is given on pages 15 and 16.

Letter forms

As in most educational matters, the experts are by no means united in their views about the correct way to form letters. It will be seen from the examples below that I align myself with those who advocate making all small letters, with the exception of 'f', 'k', 't', 'x' and 'y', with one hand movement. Of course, letters 'a' and 'g' have the simpler shapes and it is good to see that the educational publishers are also adopting the amended forms of these two letters in books for younger children.

LEARNING TO WRITE

Advice to parents on helping young children to learn to write

It is important to realise that, for most children, learning to write is linked with learning to read. All children will not be ready to learn to read and write at the same age. No two children are identical in this and pressure to learn too early can be harmful.

If, as your children grow towards school age you continue to make a habit of regularly:
  a) talking and listening to them
  b) reading aloud and sharing your pleasure in books with them
  c) providing games and materials that encourage imaginative play and the development of manipulative skills
you should be able to detect when they are ready to be helped with writing.

The making of patterns with chalks, crayons, felt pens, paint-brushes and pencils is a very good preparation for learning to write. So too, is drawing and scribbling of any kind.

Helpful patterns to introduce include:

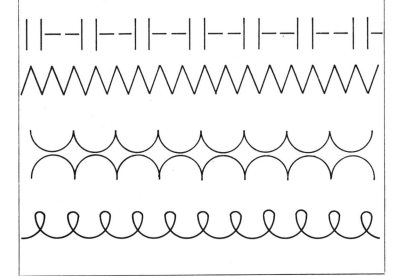

When your child does start to copy from examples you provide or from printed books, it is important to make sure that:

a) they know the 'message' of the writing (meaning and pleasure should be associated with reading and writing from the beginning)

b) they learn good habits of letter formation from the start

Small or lower-case letters are relatively more important than capital letters in the early stages and the chart below should prove helpful.

All letters are made up in one movement unless more than one arrow is numbered.

The dot beside each letter in the examples given above indicates the starting point, and the arrow shows the direction of the first stroke. Letters requiring more than one hand movement have two or three arrows. It should be emphasised that, apart from letters 'f', 'k', 't', 'x' and 'y', all letters are made without lifting the pencil from the paper during the process. It may be necessary for some children to be allowed to make letters 'd' and 'p' with two movements if they experience difficulty at first.

Relative size of lower-case letters

While it would be quite wrong to over-emphasise the importance of the relative sizes of letters in the early stages, there are generally accepted proportions and, within limits, these should be adhered to as proficiency develops.

The teacher can bring this point home to the children very simply and humorously by writing, as follows, vastly exaggerated examples and discussing them with the children.

give b.y bOat

A wall-chart showing clearly the normally accepted proportions of the letters is useful as a ready reminder of letter shapes, relative sizes and proportion of letters.

abcdefghijklmnopqrst
uvwxyz

Teaching techniques

A reception-class teacher who wants her children to learn to write print-script effectively will appreciate the need for motivating them to learn to write. She will want them to understand the function and purpose of writing. She will also be aware of the need to provide activities (such as those suggested in the previous chapter) which are designed to develop their powers of visual perception, auditory discrimination and motor co-ordination. As the children pursue these activities, the teacher will notice when some of them are sufficiently developed to be ready for instruction in handwriting skills.

Another aspect of the preparatory stage will be the deliberate attempt by the teacher to help children see the purpose of writing. She will do this through the labelling, recording and provision of simple instructions which one expects to abound in a good infants' classroom. The teacher's print-script for this display writing must be well formed since it will be the first model that most of the children will really attend to. It is a great help if the children can sometimes watch the teacher in the process of writing captions, etc.

Also during this preparatory stage, the children should be used to seeing the teacher write a sentence they have dictated under a picture they have drawn; or, as suggested in the *Breakthrough to Literacy* Teacher's Manual, forming a sentence in the 'sentence maker'. (The 'sentence maker' is a rack in which prepared cards, with words, word endings and punctuation on them, may be arranged to form sentences.) Of course it is of great importance that the first time a group of children are asked to try their hand at writing, the material is relevant and meaningful. Thus, the first-ever sentence to be attempted might well arise from a shared interest or experience, and be formed in the teacher's large sentence maker.

The first writing lessons

Assuming that these first writing lessons are to be given to a group judged to be ready, I would suggest the following course of action. First, the children should be encouraged to observe carefully while the teacher transposes the sentence from the sentence maker on to the blackboard or a large sheet of paper in well-formed print-script. As the teacher writes, and in discussion afterwards, the teacher should draw attention to:

a) the left–right writing direction
b) the spacing of letters and words
c) the relation of ascenders and descenders to the line of writing
d) most important of all, the way in which the letters are formed.

Many teachers encourage their children to join with them in forming letters in the air, and this technique can be most helpful.

The nylon-flocked 'furry' letters on the front covers of the 'letter' books in *Language in Action* (25) provide an excellent opportunity for introducing children to the shapes of letters in association with their sounds. The children should be encouraged to feel the letters with their fingertips. They need little encouragement since the texture of the letters is so inviting. However, the teacher should be watchful to see that the children learn to carry out this tactile exploration in the direction most helpful to their future writing skill needs.

Descriptive terminology

In drawing attention to the way in which letters are formed it is useful to be able to use descriptive terminology. If the children can be made familiar with such terms as 'clockwise', 'anti-clockwise', 'descender' and 'ascender', it is easier to give clear instructions and advice. A detailed example of the kind of commentary teachers give is to be found on page 52 of the Teacher's Manual to *Breakthrough to Literacy* (23). In addition, many teachers develop a personal 'fun' terminology to help enliven the hard work of learning to write. For example, Ruth Fagg in the Teacher's Book for *Everyday Writing* (7) describes the formation of letter 'r' thus:

> n is a bridge, make half a bridge r, stand on the bridge and wave goodbye r.

She describes the letter 's' thus:

> s is a graceful swan who holds her head high.

I find that the commonly used names for basic writing patterns, such as the 'bridge' pattern, the 'swings' pattern, help children appreciate their rhythmical qualities as well as the shapes. Of course the teacher will realise that the children will not absorb all these points of instruction at one telling. The aim of these first experiences and others like them is to introduce the children to the whole process in a purposeful way so that they will be motivated to pay attention to the programme of writing lessons that will follow.

Practising letter formation

The writing practice which will be needed at this stage should not be based on copying from the blackboard. Early writing copy is best provided by the teacher in the child's workbook. In this way the teacher can demonstrate size, spacing and lay-out of writing and, at the same time, relieve the child of the handicap of having to look up to the blackboard and back to the workbook. It will, however, still be useful for the teacher to write the copy on the blackboard as an additional demonstration and to facilitate group discussion. Of course, teachers will not expect perfection when children make their first attempts at copying and will be encouraging when appraising their efforts. As skills develop, copybooks and specimen cards can be used as models.

Learning the shapes and names of the letters of the alphabet will have been started already as part of the whole language arts programme, but concentration on them during the short formal lessons in writing the letters will serve to consolidate this learning. It is better to teach the shapes and methods of forming the letters in related families rather than in alphabetical order. The Platignum Instruction Copybook *Firsthand Writing* (see Aids for Teaching Handwriting, page 79), suggests an order for learning the letters which I find perfectly acceptable. The recommended order is:

    i i, t, l, formed by simple downward strokes

    ii n, m, r, h, b, p, which begin with a down-stroke followed by what may be called a bridge

    iii u begins with a swing

    iv c, a, d, g, q, o, e, formed by an anti-clockwise curve

    v v, w, y, formed by diagonal straight lines

    vi f, j, k, s, x, z, because they do not conform to any of these rules.

It is a good idea to conclude each of these brief lessons on a particular letter family or part-family by writing a sentence which incorporates several examples of the letters concerned. For example, a lesson devoted to letter 's' might be concluded by writing 'Sammy snake slept in the grass'.

Spacing

There must be some conformity in the spacing of words and lines if the writing is to be both pleasing and readable. A good working rule is to allow space for one letter ('a' or 'o') between words, and to leave sufficient space between lines so that ascenders and descenders do not overlap.

While the children are copying the writing from the copybook, card, or other model source, the teacher should be moving among them giving advice and reinforcing the main points of her teaching. She will note those children experiencing difficulty and try to find time to give them individual help so that wrong habits of letter formation will not be developed. She may have to devise special additional exercises for some children, though most of them should be able to learn to write well through the kind of teaching programme discussed.

The busy infant teacher with thirty-five or more children working an integrated day may be forgiven for asking how she will find time to give this instruction and supervision of letter-formation as well as attending to the varied needs of the rest of the class. No easy matter! But a way must be found. To fail to do so means leaving the important techniques of writing to be picked up by chance and that is not acceptable. Some teachers make use of the co-operation of other teachers, students, auxiliaries or parents to work with the rest of the class while they give their full attention to the group concerned. Others modify their organisation at certain times to make such work possible.

Additional teaching techniques for slower learners

As discussed earlier in the chapter, some children will experience difficulty in learning to write well no matter how thoughtfully the work has been prepared. For these children the following suggestions may prove useful:

a) The duplication of sheets of large-size letters formed by dots with arrows indicating the direction to be followed when joining the dots to form the letters.

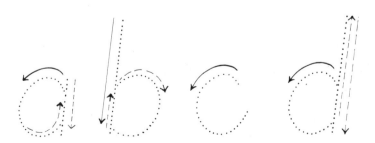

b) The use of cardboard, wooden, metal or plastic letter templates to trace over or draw round. These must be clearly marked to indicate right side up, right way round and the starting point.

c) The provision of a sheet of drawing paper on which the child sees the teacher make the letter concerned several times. The teacher adds coloured marks to indicate the starting point and direction of movement. The child then reproduces the letter many times while the teacher watches and guides.

d) Tracing with the blunt end of a pencil over a model of the letter to be learned, or using tracing paper to reproduce the letter many times. Even when children are tracing letters a watch must be kept to ensure that they form the letters using the correct movements.

e) Children experiencing difficulty over a long period and despite the provision suggested above might be helped through their tactile sense in the following ways:

i the teacher might make the letter many times over with a finger on the palm of the child's hand

ii letters can be cut out from sandpaper and stuck on card for the child to trace over with a finger – at first the child's finger should be guided by the teacher to ensure correct movements

iii letters for use in a similar way can be made by drawing with a glue pen and sprinkling on sand.

f) If the main difficulty for the child is the relationship between ascenders, descenders and the main line of writing, a frame may be helpful. This consists of three vertically-arranged rectangles into which the different parts of a letter can be fitted as shown in the diagram. Many teachers make a set of cards for all the letters of the alphabet following this pattern.

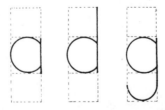

These cards can be a great help for some children. It is possible to have a rubber stamp made so that the blank frames can easily be produced for practice. Alternatively, paper may be ruled with triple lines as a temporary support for children experiencing difficulty of this kind.

Unlined paper

Although a device such as the letter-making frame can be helpful for slow-learning children, I would not advocate the use of lined paper for the majority of children learning to write. In my view, lines can be more of a hindrance than a help to the beginner since they impose yet another set of restrictions. For some children it is very difficult to make their writing 'sit' on the line. Others experience great difficulty in making the size of their letters conform to the space between the lines provided. Given plain paper and a sensibly tolerant teacher most children can obtain satisfaction from their early attempts at writing print-script. The emphasis at this stage should be on the formation of the letters, and the rest will follow.

Capital letters

Capital letters for print-script are much the same as for the Italic and Marion Richardson styles of joined writing. They should be as simple as possible and entirely devoid of flourishes and extra strokes. They should be of the same height as lower-case letters with ascenders, but will vary in width. The horizontal bar of the 'A', 'F', 'E', and 'H', is best made in line with the tops of the lower-case letters. Similarly, care must be taken over the proportions of other capitals where the danger of exaggerating one aspect must be avoided.

Width of capitals

Some capital letters fit into a square:

Some into $\frac{3}{4}$ square:

AHNTUVXYZ

Some into $\frac{1}{2}$ square:

BEFIJKLPRS

Others are based on the circle:

OQCGD

Teaching capitals

First the patterns discussed in Chapter 2 should be practised again and the descriptive terminology familiarised. Then the capital letters can be demonstrated and taught in three groups.

a) Letters made in one stroke:

b) Letters made in two strokes:

c) Letters requiring three strokes:

A series of cards showing the height, width, order and direction of stroke for each letter will be a valuable teaching aid as will a wall-chart for constant reference.

The writing tool

The main writing tool for learning print-script should be a fat, soft-lead pencil of the type commonly found in infant schools. Some practice should also be experienced with paintbrush, chalk, crayon and felt pen, etc.

Posture

Children should be encouraged to sit in a sensibly comfortable position at a table with their workbooks reasonably positioned for writing. I do not think that the acquisition of legible handwriting is facilitated by lying on the floor or sprawling in an easy chair. More formal attention to correct writing posture, if necessary, should be left to a later stage of development (see Chapter 5).

Further Reading

Gray, W. S. (14)
The author reports on his findings about the pros and cons of print-script as used in various countries.

Gourdie, T. (11)
The author points out the limitations of print-script as a precursor to a cursive hand.

Hughes, F. (18)
Chapter 7, 'Learning to Write', is interesting and controversial. A mother, who is also a teacher, describes how she taught her small daughters. Two of her recommendations are particularly controversial: (a) that the teaching of writing should not commence until the teaching of reading is finished; (b) that letters should be taught as being made up of separate components.

Mackay, D. et al. (23)
Some helpful advice on problems and techniques for the beginning stages of teaching print-script is given in Chapter 5 of the *Breakthrough to Literacy* Teacher's Manual.

Morris J. M. et al. (25)
The nylon-flocked 'furry' letters on the front covers of the letter books provide opportunities for tactile exploration of letter shapes.

The Alphabet Worksheets (three books of 30 spirit masters) provide practice in letter discrimination and in writing print-script.

4

Joined handwriting: choosing the style

Class teachers will usually be expected to teach the style of writing which has been adopted for use in their school as a whole. This may be a style with which they are not familiar. However, they will undertake this learning task willingly since they will want to present a good example of the style in question when writing on the blackboard or in a child's book. Also it would be unthinkable to allow a situation where children were required to change their style of writing at the whim of each teacher as they moved from class to class.

However, there will be occasions, perhaps in the case of a new school or if the staff of a school are dissatisfied with the standard of handwriting being achieved, when all available styles will be examined and compared with a view to selecting one for adoption. Accordingly, it is useful to discuss and illustrate the alternatives and to list the teaching materials available for use in teaching each style.

In my view, three main styles should be considered – namely, cursive, Italic and Marion Richardson. Unfortunately, there appears to be some confusion about the precise meaning of the term 'cursive'. The *Shorter Oxford English Dictionary* defines cursive as 'written with a running hand so that characters are rapidly formed without raising the pen'. Yet, to accept this definition is to exclude such styles as Italic and Marion Richardson which, though they are certainly running hands, do allow for certain breaks.

For each of these three styles there is an enthusiastic band of supporters. The fervour with which they champion their particular style is in sharp contradiction to the lack of knowledge and interest in the skill of handwriting which critics of progressive education claim to be characteristic of the majority of teachers and college of education lecturers. There are also at least three other styles worthy of mention – the Round Style, Everyday Writing and Firsthand Writing.

Cursive writing

Cursive writing is characterised by the joining of letters with loops. Modern-day versions of the style are derived from the 'Copperplate' or 'civil service' style and critics complain that, even in the simplified adaptations in use today, the written characters are not sufficiently similar to their printed counterparts. In consequence, children are obliged to learn two forms of some letters. Cursive writing is also criticised because of its tendency to deteriorate when written at speed. It becomes less legible and certainly less aesthetically pleasing when the looped ascenders and descenders are not uniform in shape, size and angle. However, advocates of the style claim that many children and parents consider cursive writing to be the only 'real' writing. They argue that children are motivated to make greater efforts to master the style as it represents an aspect of 'growing up', whereas this motivational factor is not experienced when children learn what is termed 'joint-script'.

Example of the cursive style

*I too will something make
And joy in the making;
Altho' to-morrow it seem
Like the empty words of a dream
Remembered on waking.*

Robert Bridges

Italic writing

Italic writing was developed during the Renaissance and many versions of the style have since evolved. Some of the main characteristics of italic are the narrow curving bends, the narrowed eliptical letter shapes, the slope of the writing and the 'thicks' and 'thins' which result from the correct angling of a blunt-ended, non-flexible nib. Critics of the style claim that it is precious, slow and without individuality. Its supporters naturally refute these charges, and they are numerous and enthusiastic enough to have formed a Society for Italic Handwriting. Indeed, they claim that the Italic style has many virtues – grace and beauty, legibility and rhythmical pattern. However, advocates of Italic writing do concede that at the learning practice stage there is a certain laborious uniformity. But they point out that once a basic style is mastered and the learner writes at speed, he enjoys the freedom to develop individual variations which lead to the development of a personal Italic handwriting style.

Examples of Italic styles

Earth has not anything to show more fair :
Dull would he be of soul who could pass by
A sight so touching in its majesty:
This City now doth, like a garment, wear
The beauty of the morning; silent, bare,
Ships, towers, domes, theatres, & temples lie
Open unto the fields, and to the sky;
All bright and glittering in the smokeless air.
Never did sun more beautifully steep
In its first splendour, valley, rock, or hill;
Ne'er saw I, never felt, a calm so deep!
The river glideth at his own sweet will:

Beacon Handwriting

45 Castle Road Bridgetown
30th. December 1961

Dear Mary,

Since I last wrote to you I have
been learning to write quickly and well
with a square-edged pen.

You will see that only some of the
letters in words are joined. Joins are used
only when they help us to write letters
together quickly and easily in one smooth
movement. I have also been learning how

The Teaching of Handwriting

God be in my head
And in my Understanding.
God be in my eyes
And in my Looking.
God be in my mouth
And in my Speaking.
God be in my heart

Italic Platignum

29 JOINED HANDWRITING: CHOOSING THE STYLE

Though I speak with the tongues of men and
of angels, and have not charity, I am become
as sounding brass or a tinkling cymbal.
And though I have the gift of prophecy, and
understand all mysteries and all knowledge;
and though I have all faith, so that I could
remove mountains, and have not charity,
I am nothing.
And though I bestow all my goods to feed the
poor; and though I give my body to be burned,
and have not charity, it profiteth me nothing.

Osmiroid Italic

From about the third century BC
the instrument mainly used for
writing on papyrus was the reed-
pen. This was a length of common
reed; at first the writing end was
frayed or pulped; later it was cut
to a point and split and then sharp-
ened with a knife. The quill, made
from the wing-feathers of geese,
swans, peacocks, or eventually tur-
keys, was in use from the Middle
Ages to the nineteenth century.

I Can Write

There seems to have been very little research comparing hand-writing styles but a limited study is reported by George L. Thomson in *Scottish Educational Journal*, June 1954 (35). The pupils in four schools each using a different style of writing were asked to write for two minutes in three separate ways: their very best writing for a sentence copied down; as much as they could when writing an ordinary letter; and as much as they could when using their fastest scribble. Examination of the results led to the conclusion that, even at speed, the Italic examples were legible and good to look at, and that Italic was 6.4 per cent faster than any other style. These findings tend to refute the critics of Italic writing.

One recent Italic scheme that may be of particular interest to teachers using informal teaching approaches is *I Can Write* by Tom Gourdie (13), who is also the author of *A Guide to Better Handwriting* (11). His *Simple Modern Hand* (12) was first introduced into Edinburgh schools and was illustrated on eight sets of cards (The *Gourdie Italic Handwriting Cards*, published by Holmes McDougall), and in a series of three books (published by Collins). When the original cards and books were devised they were appropriate to the needs of children in the class-teaching situations which generally prevailed. Now Tom Gourdie, in the *I Can Write* scheme, has devised approaches and materials based on the same pure movements and simple shapes but necessitating very little supervision when children are actually working from the materials. In other words, he has revised his original scheme to facilitate learning to write in an integrated-day classroom.

Tom Gourdie's suggestions for classroom organisation include opportunities for practising handwriting skills through his book-lets, stencil masters of patterns and letter forms, instructional flash cards and practice books. But he also emphasises, as I have done, the positive role of the teacher. He suggests that it will be necessary for teachers to spend time ensuring that children form good sitting habits, that they hold the writing tool correctly, position the paper properly and that they fully understand how to use the materials.

I would reiterate that teachers will still need to keep a watchful eye on the children's efforts to prevent the development of bad habits. Of course, this is true of most classroom activities. The *I Can Write* materials should certainly help increase the success rate considerably.

The Marion Richardson style

The Marion Richardson style of handwriting was developed in the nineteen-thirties by the brilliant LCC Art Inspector of that name. The style is based on easy and natural movements of arm and hand for small children which result in more rounded letter-shapes in comparison with the more oval shapes of Italic letters. The making of rhythmical patterns even before the child is ready to take an interest in letters is a strong feature of the scheme and the enjoyment of creating patterns is encouraged throughout the course. As will be seen below, the Marion Richardson style is also characterised by the open letters 'p' and 'b' which allow for joins from these letters to be more easily made, and a rounded version of the letters 'f', 'k', 'w', 'x', 'y', 'z'. With these exceptions, the letter forms are very similar to those used in the simplified print used in reading books for young children.

Example of Marion Richardson style

Years afterwards she could bring the
whole scene back again, as if it had
been only yesterday —the mild blue
eyes & kindly smile of the Knight —the
setting sun gleaming through his hair,
& shining on his armour in a blaze of
light that quite dazzled her—the horse
quietly moving about, with the reins
hanging loose on his neck, cropping the
grass at her feet —& the black shadows
behind—all this she took in like a picture,
as, with one hand shading her eyes,

Marion Richardson intended that children should learn to write her style from the beginning without going through a phase of writing print-script. Children who have learned to write in schools adhering to this principle seem to have achieved a very satisfactory standard of handwriting without experiencing the problems over print in reading books which some teachers fear are inevitable.

Alternative styles

The three other styles mentioned, the Round Style, Everyday Writing and Firsthand Writing, are all styles that seem to have been developed by educators in an attempt to help children develop a clear, legible style of joined-script writing from the familiar letter-forms of print-script. A complete course of learning is provided for these three styles and the end product in each case certainly appears to be pleasant and legible.

Example of Round Style

Forth into the forest highway
All alone walked Hiawatha
Proudly, with his bows and arrows;
And the birds sang round him, o'er him,
'Do not shoot us, Hiawatha!'
Sang the robin, the Opechee,
Sang the bluebird, the Owaissa,
'Do not shoot us, Hiawatha!'

Example of Everyday Writing

For, lo, the winter is past, the rain is over
   and gone;
The flowers appear on the earth;
The time of the singing of birds is come,
And the voice of the turtle is heard
   in our land;
The figtree putteth forth her green figs,
And the vines with the tender grape
   give a good smell.

Example of Firsthand Writing

Four ducks on a pond,
A grass bank beyond,
A blue sky of spring,
White clouds on the wing;
What a little thing
To remember for years –
To remember with tears.

Recommendation based on experience

The styles of writing discussed above are the main ones for which teaching materials and guides are available. The choice is one of personal preference but, hopefully, this guide will help to make the choice an informed one. My choice of style involves a combination of approaches for the following reasons. I believe that the Marion Richardson style, with its rounded forms and strong rhythmical quality is the most suitable style of joined-script for small children to learn. I also believe that print-script with its concentration on individual letter formation and its uncluttered correspondence to print in early readers is beneficial for most children at the early stages of becoming literate. Therefore, I favour introducing children to the basic Marion Richardson patterns from the beginning. This pattern-making helps to develop motor co-ordination and provides experience of the cursive nature of handwriting as well as giving pleasure through the exploration of shape, rhythm and colour. When the child is ready to take a more formal interest in letters, I suggest teaching the correct way to make well formed print-script while continuing with the pattern work. Then, when the print-script letter shapes have been thoroughly mastered and the basic patterns confidently and fluently achieved, I suggest that teaching of the Marion Richardson writing should begin. This stage might be reached at top infant or first-year junior level and, in my view, the learning and practice should continue till about the third-year junior level.

At this stage in children's development, the muscular skills have matured to a point at which the elliptical shapes of Italic writing are no longer unnatural, and the children themselves may feel that their Marion Richardson hand is immature. This is the time to interest the children in one of the Italic styles, or in modifying their Marion Richardson writing. Moreover, my experience indicates that, not only is this transition easily accomplished, but it provides a fresh stimulus to the children who can then usually be encouraged to develop a satisfactory personal Italic handwriting before leaving the primary school for secondary school.

Materials for teaching joined handwriting

a) Teaching materials for cursive writing

i Copy books 1-8 by Vere Foster (Blackie)
ii Aids from Platignum Ltd
Instruction sheet no. 1 (free); Copy book – Cursive; Wall-chart – Cursive.
iii Aids from E. S. Perry Ltd (Osmiroid)
Handwriting Aid Sheet no. 1 (free); Wall-chart – Cursive.

b) Teaching materials for Italic writing

i The Teaching of Handwriting by A. Inglis and E. Gibson (Nelson)
Infant Scheme – Work Books A and B; Teachers' Manual (19)
Primary Scheme – Work Books 1-4; Teachers' Manual (20)
ii Beacon Writing edited by A. Fairbank (Ginn)
Books 1-6; Supplement to Books 1 and 2; Teacher's Book for books 1 and 2 (33)
iii Renaissance Italic Handwriting Books by W. Worthy (Chatto & Windus)
A set of four books for children.
iv The Gourdie Italic Handwriting Cards by Tom Gourdie (Holmes McDougall) 1956
A series of eight sets of cards (A–H) giving complete instruction in Italic writing.
v The Simple Modern Hand by Tom Gourdie (Collins) (12)
A series of three children's books plus a teacher's book provides complete instruction in a modified Italic hand.
vi Quick and Legible Handwriting by D. Fletcher, R. Bakewell and N. K. Robertson (Oliver & Boyd)
A series of five books for children and a Teacher's Manual (9).
vii Italic Copybooks by David Horsburgh (Oxford University Press)
A series of five books providing a complete course in Italic handwriting.
viii Aids from Platignum Ltd
Italic Copybook; Italic Wall-chart; Instruction Sheet no. 3 (free).

ix Aids from E. S. Perry Ltd (Osmiroid)
Italic Wall-chart; 'The Osmiroid Guide to Italic Handwriting' (free); Handwriting Aid Sheet no. 3 (free); Film-loop – 'How to Write Well'.
x Aids from Dryad Ltd
Film-strip – 'The Development of Italic Handwriting'.

c) Teaching materials for Marion Richardson writing

i Writing and Writing Patterns, by Marion Richardson (University of London Press)
Booklets A and B; Books 1–5; Books 1–5 in card form; Teacher's Book (30).
ii Aids from E. S. Perry Ltd (Osmiroid)
Marion Richardson Wall-chart; Handwriting Aid Sheet no. 2 (free).

d) Teaching materials for the Round Style

Aids from Platignum Ltd
Round Style Wall-chart; Round Style Copybook; Instruction Sheet no. 2 (free).

e) Teaching materials for Everyday Writing

Everyday Writing Scheme by Ruth Fagg (University of London Press)
Books 1–5; Teacher's Book (7).

f) Teaching materials for Firsthand Writing

Aids from Platignum Ltd
Firsthand Writing Copybook.

g) Teaching materials for I Can Write

I Can Write by Tom Gourdie and Delia Atkinson (Macmillan) (13)
The materials include tracing cards, spirit duplicator sheets and copying booklets organised in five development stages and providing a comprehensive introduction to the Simple Modern Hand style of writing.

h) *Writemaster Books 4–6* (43) by P. Smith and J. Williams (Holmes McDougall. Three books of spirit masters containing exercises designed to facilitate learning the Marion Richardson style of writing at the same time as spelling. Notes of guidance for children and teachers are provided.

i) *Write and Spell* (45) by Joyce and Peter Young (Oliver and Boyd). A series of four expendable workbooks for learning to write and spell at the same time. The cursive writing style has been designed by the addition of simple ligatures to the print script the children already know.

Further Reading

Gourdie, T. (11)
Many of the alternative styles are described and advice on teaching techniques given. The author discusses their merits and demerits and provides copious illustrations.

Thomson, G. L. (35)
Legibility at speed in various writing styles is discussed in *Italic Handwriting for Schools*.

5

Teaching joined writing

Preparation for learning

Most children should be writing adequately in print-script before
they leave the infant school, and many 7-year-olds will be capable
of writing pleasant print-script at a good speed. These top infants,
or first-year junior children, are the pupils who will be ready to
begin a course designed to facilitate the change-over to a joined
style of handwriting. At this stage it should be possible and
expedient to give the necessary initial instruction to a fairly large
group.

The course of instruction should begin with the demonstration
and study of an example of the style of joined writing to be learned.
Ideally, this will have been decided as a matter of school policy.

The group of children concerned should be encouraged to
observe and discuss the differences they notice between a passage
written in the chosen joined style and the same passage written in
the familiar print-script. They should be told that they will
gradually be taught the correct method of achieving the joined
style and that, in the meantime, they are to continue with print-
script for all written work except the special writing lessons. It is
not advisable to allow children to attempt to reproduce the style
before being taught the techniques involved in its execution.

The detailed suggestions outlined below are in accordance with
the particular style preference already discussed in the final
paragraphs of chapter 4. However, with some modification, the
recommendations should be relevant to any style.

One essential is to create a renewed interest in writing patterns, with a particular emphasis on rhythm, speed and fluency. Experimenting by interweaving various patterns and elaborating the resulting design engenders fresh enthusiasm. Much of the pattern-making at this stage could be of normal writing size, and the practice of drawing a band of pattern to decorate a page of work provides additional practice as well as increasing the sense of pleasure and pride in achievement. The use of colour provides further incentive.

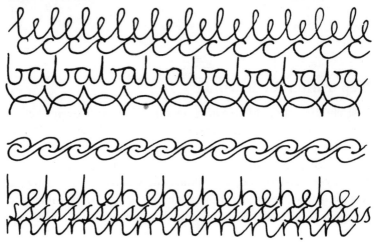

Teaching ligaturing

In all styles of joined handwriting it is necessary to demonstrate and provide practice in the various ligaturing techniques. For some styles, it is recommended that finished forms of letters including entry and exit strokes should be learned before commencing ligaturing. The relevant teacher's manual should be consulted in this connexion, and also to ascertain those letters of the alphabet which take an amended form. For example, in Marion Richardson the following amendments must be learned:

$$b\ p\ k\ f\ s\ s\ w\ x\ y\ 3$$

It must be pointed out that there are two forms of letter 's': the traditional form usually being used at the beginnings of words only, and the amended form being used after a ligature. Although some people, including children, when writing at speed, make a join following the letter 's' with reasonable success, it is not generally recommended. The normal practice is to break after letter 's' because there is not an incipient ligature and attempts to join may result in ugly shapes.

Because one of the fundamental qualities of a running hand is movement, the writer favours teaching children to join from the exit point of one letter to the entry point of the next in one rhythmical flowing movement without first learning the 'finished' forms of letters. This approach is in accordance with the procedures recommended in the Teacher's Book for the Marion Richardson style (30). Initial practice in ligaturing is best arranged by grouping letters according to the direction of the ligature. The first technique to be acquired is the diagonal join from letters which finish with a low right-side exit to letters which commence with a high left-side entry but have no ascenders.

It is absolutely essential that these diagonal ligatures are always made at the same angle, otherwise the letters will not be uniformly spaced.

GROUP I. Letters with a low right-side exit point:

*a c d e h i k l m
n p t u x z*

Note that the letters in group I above do not include the 'z' in the Marion Richardson style.

GROUP 2. Letters with a high left-side entry point but without ascenders on the left:

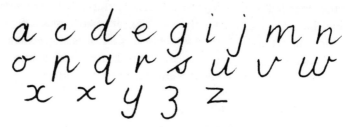

Letters in group 1 may be diagonally linked to any letter in group 2, and the children should practise linking them in pairs and exploring the possible permutations.

ac de mu ti ls

GROUP 3. It will be noticed that the following letters occur in both groups 1 and 2:

a c d e i m n u p

These letters have both a low right exit point and a high left entry point and may therefore be joined continuously or in a variety of clusters thus:

acdei mnu acm emn

Children will enjoy a game in which they find words which can be formed from the eight letters in group 3 and which they can write without breaks.

acid mine din aim

GROUP 4. A fourth group to be considered are those letters with a left-side ascender:

$$b \; \mathit{b} \; f \; f \; h \; k \; l \; t$$

Any letter with a low right-side exit (those in group 1) may be joined to these but, in order that the angle of diagonal and the space between letters may remain uniform, the point of entry to these letters is at mid-point on the ascender. In the case of letter 't' it will be two-thirds up.

$$ab \quad ch \quad mk \quad nl \quad ef$$

GROUP 5. The next group of letters to receive attention should be those after which a horizontal join occurs:

$$b \; f \; f \; o \; r \; v \; w$$

Practice will be needed in joining on from these letters to all other letters; those in group 2 should be tackled first because the ligature will indeed be horizontal.

$$bn \quad va \quad wo \quad om \quad rn$$

Next those in group 4 should be practised because the ligature will now be diagonal to the top of the ascender. Moreover, the angle of the diagonal must remain constant and uniform with all other diagonal ligatures.

$$ob \quad vl \quad rh \quad wf \quad ff$$

GROUP 6. The final group of letters to be considered contains those after which a break occurs:

$$g \; j \; y \; 3 \; q \; b \; p$$

The four letters with curved descenders are only ever joined on in the looped cursive style. Any attempt to join on from them in non-looped styles results in rather ugly shapes at the best, and hideous forms at worst.

get girl jump

In most non-looped styles no join is made after letters 'b' and 'p' for similar reasons but ligatures are easily made from the open 'b' and 'p' of Marion Richardson. Most teachers would include 's' in the list of letters requiring breaks but, as already stated, others would make joins after 's' quite happily to achieve greater speed and accuracy.

rusty straw dress ash

Capital letters and ligaturing

In general, capital letters should not be joined to any other letter. The Copperplate style is one exception.

Use of copybooks and other models

Once the various ligaturing techniques have been taught and sufficient practice has led to reasonable proficiency, use can be made of prepared copybooks and cards, etc. Attention should be drawn to the writing size, spacing and layout of the writing models, and the children should be encouraged to develop good habits of general presentation throughout their copy work. It is therefore important that all models provided for copying should excel in these matters as well as in letter shapes and ligatures. The following points need to be borne in mind:

a) Any writing copy should be placed above the book or paper rather than by the side. It is better for the writer to have to look up at the copy and back down to the book than move the head from side to side.

b) The copybooks and model cards supplied with a writing scheme are usually arranged in progression, and children must be supplied with material appropriate to their needs and stage of development.

c) It is important that a child is able to read, or at least has had read to him, any passage he is set to copy. The fact that handwriting is a vehicle for verbal communication must not be overlooked in the process of teaching the mechanical skill.

d) Additional practice based on models can now be profitably encouraged in spare time at school or at home. This would not have been so prior to the course of instruction in ligaturing.

e) The teacher must continue to be on the alert for children who may have failed to master or remember any of the techniques, or who may regress and start to develop bad writing habits.

f) The teacher will want to encourage, praise, correct or reprimand a pupil according to his degree of success, application and effort. A thoughtful teacher will appreciate the problems of children with weak muscular co-ordination or poor visual discrimination and will provide additional help and support. The teacher will be careful not to discourage such children who are really trying, but will be ready to take a different line with those who fail to make a genuine effort. As in most teaching situations, a positive approach is most likely to produce good results, and warm praise for achievement and effort coupled with display of good examples of children's work should serve to encourage most children in the group.

The writing instrument

As in most teaching situations, there is no generally accepted view about which instrument to use at various stages. What follows are my personal preferences and my reasons for them.

a) In the beginning stages when young children are enjoying pattern-making and learning to form print-script, I advocate the use of a thick soft-lead pencil as the main writing tool, although brush, crayon, chalk, felt-pen, etc., will also be suitable and provide varied experience.

b) At upper infant or lower junior level, when print-script is being perfected and joined writing introduced, I recommend the standard school black-lead pencil (HB). Too hard a pencil is unsatisfactory and too soft a pencil, though making a most satisfactory black mark, is uneconomic and requires too frequent sharpening.

c) Towards the end of the second-year junior stage, I like to introduce pen and ink. The preferred nib is stiff, square-cut and with the writing edge slightly turned up if possible so that it writes smoothly. A medium-width italic nib is suitable and is available from several firms. Moreover, although I think all children should have some experience with dip pens, one must accept that the fountain pen has largely superseded them. Accordingly, the majority of children can reasonably be encouraged to acquire low-priced fountain pens with suitable nibs. (Several manufacturing companies produce quite good quality fountain pens at a reasonable price.)

d) The ball-point pen is now widely used and accepted. As a writing instrument for everyday classwork it has the advantage over a pencil that it does not need sharpening and will write equally clearly and speedily without the exertion of pressure. Therefore it must be admitted to school, but not to the exclusion of the nibbed pen. In my view, for formal writing practice, written work to be displayed, etc., a nibbed pen is essential. In fact, immense pleasure and pride is to be gained from well-formed writing executed with the right instrument.

Pen or pencil hold

Since the aim is to achieve fluent, easy, unconscious skill in handwriting, teachers will not want to restrict their pupils by an undue emphasis on a particular pen grip or posture. Yet they will want to make sure that the children do not develop bad habits that will handicap their efforts. Any pen hold that is comfortable for the child and yet permits correct hand movement and shape formation with a pen is acceptable to me, but the following points form the basis of advice I would give to a child experiencing difficulty over grip.

a) The pen or pencil is best held lightly between thumb and forefinger, about one inch from the point, with the middle finger providing additional support. The other two fingers are not involved in the process and can rest lightly on the paper along with the side of the hand.

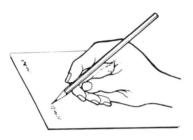

b) The pen or pencil should point along the line of the forearm to the right of the shoulder.

c) The angle of the pen to the plane of the paper should be approximately 45°. The angle to the line of writing should also be 45° at the beginning of the writing line, but this angle will decrease as the hand progresses along the line.

In a sense, it is unfortunate that reasonably successful writing can be achieved with a pencil no matter how it is held. Unless the teacher is watchful in the early stages, a habit of holding the pencil in a wrong manner may be formed and this could lead to much difficulty when the habit has to be broken and a new grip learned. Some teachers see this as a reason for introducing the pen early in order to confront the children with the imperative need for correct pen hold.

Left-handed children

The advice given above applies to right-handed children; the problems of the left-handed child are quite different. It is generally accepted that no action should be taken to effect a change of hand in pupils in whom left-handed dominance is firmly established, but they clearly need special help since they cannot be allowed to write from right to left as would be natural for them.

A thorough consideration of the writing difficulties of left-handed children, together with helpful teaching suggestions, is to be found in *Teaching Left-handed Children* (4). Margaret Clark, the author, emphasises the importance of instructing left-handed children in the correct position of the paper, a suitable type of pen and the correct grip.

Advice on pen hold for left-handed writers

a) Method of grip is the same as for right-handers except that the pen or pencil should be held further away from the point. This is necessary for the writer to see what he has written and to avoid smudging ink. Left-handed children are particularly prone to grip the pen or pencil too tightly.

b) The angle of the pen to the plane of the paper will be more difficult to achieve and specially angled nibs for left-handed writers are available.

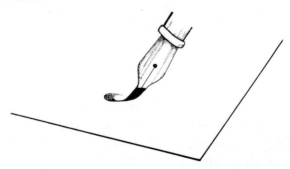

c) Diagonal ligatures will involve pushing instead of pulling unless the wrist is twisted so that the pen is at the same angle as for the right-hander. The alternative to this is to use a smooth, rounded nib which may be pushed without digging into the paper but will not produce shaded writing.

Posture

The most significant factor in posture is the furniture. A child must be seated comfortably at a table or desk of the correct height on a chair of the correct height. This can be easily checked. If the writing surface is the right height it will allow the forearm to be supported parallel to the ground. Too high a table will cause the forearm to incline upwards and too low a writing surface will have the opposite effect. The height of the seat should be such that the child's thighs are horizontal and the feet flat on the floor. Too often in schools one finds children sitting at tables or on chairs of the wrong height. In view of the variety of height to be found in any age-group, the common practice of furnishing a classroom with a uniform size of furniture may not be helpful in the achievement of good handwriting.

Provided with suitable furniture, the child should be encouraged to sit straight with elbows just to the side of the body. The writing paper should be placed slightly to the right of a line with the centre of the body and be parallel to the edge of the desk or tilted slightly to the left. For a left-handed child the paper should be placed slightly to the left of a line with the centre of the body and be parallel to the edge of the desk or tilted slightly to the right.

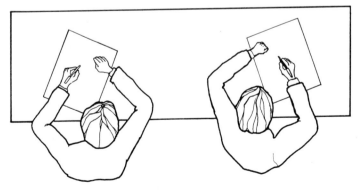

It is an obvious advantage if the source of light is on the left of a right-handed child and on the right of a left-handed child, but it is not realistic to expect this to be possible for every child in the classroom. Fortunately sunlight does not create shadows of an intensity to disturb the writer, but it is important that artificial lighting is so arranged that disconcerting shadows are not thrown on to the writing surfaces.

Lined or unlined paper

Another controversial issue is the use of lined or unlined paper. Many experts take the view that lined paper is essential for a child to write straight and in an acceptable size. It is considered that the lines serve as direction indicators and minimum and maximum height controls. Some teachers go even further and advocate groups of lines like music staves so that the proportions of ascenders and descenders are also rigidly controlled. Another school of thought sees lines as direction indicators and boundaries within which the child is free to decide the size of the writing.

An opposite point of view is taken by those who feel that lines can be a handicap to a child in the early stages of learning to write, in that the spacing of the lines predetermines the size of writing, compelling an unnatural and undesirable conformity. The opponents of lined paper also feel that the obligation on the child to make the writing 'sit' on the line puts an additional unnecessary burden on the small child who needs to be able to concentrate on making correct letter forms.

My personal preference is for unlined paper in the early stages of learning to write, for the reasons set out in the previous paragraph, although I concede that a very small minority of children may need the prop of guidelines. (See Chapter 7 for more details.) However, in due course, children should be taught to write confidently on both lined and unlined paper. Therefore when enough efficiency in the skill has been achieved, they should be introduced to wide-spaced lined paper as supplied for use by infants.

In teaching the use of lined paper I recommend that writing is made to 'sit' on the line, that capital letters and ascenders reach up to the line above and descenders halfway down to the line below.

Although I would want to ensure that my pupils were able to write comfortably on lined and unlined paper, I prefer to use plain paper for the majority of hand-writing lessons, and when presentation pieces are being executed. Unlined paper has the advantage of allowing the writer to determine the size of writing, spacing, arrangement of the page, and relationship of writing to illustration. It sets a child free to create an aesthetic whole which enhances the feelings of pride and pleasure for the writer. I am also firmly convinced that well-formed handwriting is more pleasing against a plain background than against lines. Furthermore, I have satisfied myself time and again that very few children experience difficulty in writing in reasonably straight lines on plain paper.

Further Reading

Clark, M. (4)
A report on an investigation into the problems of left-handed children in Scotland.

Fagg, R. (7)
The author describes effective techniques and approaches for the teaching of joined handwriting.

Gourdie, T. (11)
The technique of handwriting and the teaching of handwriting are dealt with (pages 55–67), and writing equipment is discussed (pages 67–73).

Inglis, A. and Gibson, E. (20)
The authors provide detailed advice for teacher and pupils for their Italic scheme.

Richardson, M. (30)
Marion Richardson provides comprehensive guidance for teaching the patterns and style she devised.

Stone, C. (33)
Particularly helpful with advice for the beginning stages of learning to write Italic.

6

Maintaining and improving standards of handwriting

If the teaching of handwriting is done well in the primary school by teachers pursuing a common school policy there is no reason why the vast majority of children should not be writing a satisfactory joined hand by the age of 9. However, in addition to those children who fail to reach an acceptable standard because of physical problems or poor attitudes, there will inevitably be some whose failure is due to lack of continuity in tuition, in these times of mobility among both teachers and taught.

It must consequently be accepted that there will continue to be a need to teach handwriting to some children in the older classes of the junior school and even in the secondary school. There is no place for the attitude that teachers of 10-year-olds and above have no responsibility for teaching basic skills. Those teachers of middle-school age children who do accept the need to continue teaching handwriting to the poor writers in their class will probably prefer to devise an individual course based on the principles discussed in previous chapters, and the special comments that will be included in Chapter 7 for those pupils with severe learning impediments.

This chapter, in the main, is devoted to considering the need for and provision of revision, together with a discussion of motivation and incentives for children to develop a personal style based on the style taught in the school. The reader will recall that towards the end of Chapter 4 I discussed my belief that, at about the age of 10, children's muscular powers have developed to a point at which elliptical shapes are not unnatural, and many children become interested in developing a more mature style. The transition from Marion Richardson to a form of Italic, or a modified Marion Richardson, at this stage is a very easy one and provides fresh enthusiasm at a time when interest in handwriting might well be flagging.

One practical problem is that of the youngster who comes into a class with a mastery of a handwriting style other than the one taught in the school. The busy teacher who manages to include occasional class revision lessons to prevent regression may not have time to provide similar revision in the appropriate style for the newcomer. There will not be the same urgency to provide special individual writing lessons as there is for the poor writer. There might well be a temptation to get the newcomer to change to the school style, but that would cause at least temporary regression and affect his work in other subjects. What then is to be done? My feeling is that if a newcomer has an adequate mastery of a different style he should be allowed to retain and develop it. Copybooks and other model sources should be made available for individual revision and practice, with the teacher giving general encouragement.

Revision

At the top end of the primary school the focus in written expression will be more and more on the quality of the content, and our aim is to help the children achieve an unconscious skill in handwriting which relieves them of the need to think about it. Handwriting must be legible if it is to communicate, and it should be pleasing in appearance. Indeed, a general pride in the total finished written piece is indicative of an attitude which makes for all-round quality. Older junior children may be presented with the idea that we each have three standards of writing as follows:

a) Our conscious best, when we devote our maximum attention to the mechanical skill. We can only hope to achieve this standard when freed from the other demands of written expression – composition, content, grammar and spelling. Therefore this standard of excellence will only be attempted in actual handwriting exercises or when copying out a draft piece for presentation. It is not to be expected in ordinary written expression work. The attempt would slow down the flow of creative thought, and the more important aspects of written expression would suffer through neglect.

b) A reasonable legible standard which can be achieved at satisfactory speed and without demanding much concentration from the writer. Naturally, this everyday standard of handwriting will itself improve as a result of the occasional handwriting lesson.

c) Scribble or carelessly formed writing which should never be tolerated. It reflects a lack of interest and pride and the children must know it will not be acceptable. Of course, teachers must be sure they are just and sensible in this matter. Moreover, the decision as to what is acceptable must be made with reference to the ability of the individual, and not to a so-called class norm.

No matter how well children have been taught to write, with faithful adherence to the characteristics of the particular style, regressions will occur through carelessness or outside influences. The desire to imitate some of the flourishes in a relative's or friend's handwriting is understandable. Indeed, some teachers feel that children should be allowed to experiment quite freely with any style or combination of styles. However, if the reader agrees with me that children are best served by being encouraged to develop an individual style based on logical principles, then it is essential to provide periodic revision until the principles of the style are firmly established.

Of course, there are many ways of providing the necessary revision. A chart showing the letter shapes and various ligatures should always be available. When the teacher notices a fault in handwriting, the child can then be encouraged to refer to the chart to discover the nature of the fault before undertaking some of the individual practice designed to eradicate it.

Occasional large group or whole class revision lessons are essential. These lessons can be based on the teaching techniques described in Chapter 5, but a fresh approach to the same learning task is often appreciated. One such variation is to consider the letters of the alphabet as 'families' according to the basic movement with which they are made. This involves the teacher writing on the blackboard a line of basic writing pattern and then establishing with the children which letters belong to the family. Practice in joining the 'members of the family' is then undertaken, with the order of the letters changed to provide a variety of ligatures. The revision exercise is completed by composing together a sentence in which the family letters are liberally featured.

cccccccccc

a c d e g o q

A good dog lived in
a palace with a queen.

nmmmmmm

n m r h k p b p

nmrh kpbr mrhp

His father took him to
the park.

uuuuuuuu

v u i t l y w b

uitly wilt bully

They built the wall
with yellow bricks.

These three patterns, the C, the bridges and the swings, are the basis of the three main families and give rise to twenty-one of the twenty-six letters. The other five letters must be treated separately, but the following pattern rhythm from the Marion Richardson style is helpful with regard to

s f j x 3

The suggestions outlined above for revising letter shapes and ligatures through the family approach have been made in a general manner. The teacher's manual for the particular handwriting style being taught should be consulted for more specific guidance.

Incentive for practice of handwriting

Today's teachers are only too well aware of the amount of written expression produced by the older juniors in lively schools. The children write copiously to produce stories, reports, written work on topics, plays and poems. However, in this kind of work the emphasis is on the content and an insistence on immaculate handwriting would be inhibiting. What is needed in addition to the formal revision and corrective exercises discussed above are occasional purposeful opportunities for writing of presentation standard.

When children are writing out pieces for presentation in this way, the opportunity occurs to draw attention to the aesthetic aspects of layout. Discussion and consideration of side margin widths and the relative proportions of top and bottom margins should be encouraged. Many of the authors of books on caligraphy deal with this subject fully, and the reader will probably have personal preferences. There is no need for conformity of practice. The aim should be to get children thinking about such matters. Thought must also be given to the arrangement of illustrations in the books they produce.

The following ways of purposefully encouraging careful presentation have been found useful.

a) Letters

Generally, children no longer learn how to write letters through sterile exercises in their books. The letters which they write to exchange news with other children, to say thank you, to request help and information or for whatever other purposes, present an excellent opportunity for practice. The content of the letter will be drafted and looked over by the teacher before the writing commences so that the child is free to concentrate on the techniques. The pupil is motivated to excel because the letter will be received and read by the addressee.

b) Anthologies

Children enjoy making anthologies of favourite poems and short extracts of prose. Once the child has made the selection, complete concentration on the aesthetic aspects of presentation is possible. Additional decoration through illustration and bands of writing pattern all serve to increase pride and pleasure.

c) Magazines and wall displays

Contributions will be of the children's own composition, but they should be drafted, and then looked over by the teacher or editor so that the task of copying out for presentation is a purely aesthetic one. If the standard of presentation of visual aids and reports on topics, etc., is normally good in the classroom the children will want their work to be of equal excellence and will have the incentive to write really well. It is, of course, essential that due notice of the wall display or magazine is taken. The head-teacher has an important part to play in this respect, but colleagues and other classes can be invited to share the pleasure and interest.

Apart from fair copies of letters and items for exhibition in group magazines and wall displays, I do not favour the practice of children copying out their work a second time. The incentive to continue making writing patterns can be provided through their use to decorate programmes and catalogues, etc. They can also be used most effectively to enhance the appearance of clay models, or as space-fillers on outline drawings, as well as being painted as bases for wallpaper and fabric design.

Changing from Marion Richardson to Italic handwriting

Some teachers of older juniors may consider it desirable that their pupils change over from the Marion Richardson to an Italic style of handwriting. In which case I suggest that the children are first shown an example or various examples of Italic styles followed by discussion of the basic differences. The teacher's manual for the Italic style will naturally prove a source of information upon which the teacher can base the advice and exercises necessary to facilitate change. Workbooks or other models at the appropriate level are useful so that children may have guided practice at school and at home based on the principles they have already thoroughly absorbed.

Alternatively, pupils can be simply encouraged to modify the letter shapes of Marion Richardson style to a more elliptical form, which will result in letter forms being less wide. If at the same time the slope to the right is introduced or increased slightly the resultant writing will have a more mature appearance.

Whichever style is chosen as the basis for this final stage of development in writing, and even if the school policy has been to follow a particular writing scheme throughout the primary years, the upper-junior years are the time when children should be encouraged to develop their own personal style soundly based on what they have been taught.

Further Reading

Inglis, A. and Gibson, E. (20)
The authors give advice on illustrated capitals, layout of writing. letter writing etc. (page 97).

Marshall, S. (24)
The author describes the practice of allowing children to write 'first drafts' of their creative writing which are then used for handwriting practice and decorating in readiness for display (pages 50–2).

7

Diagnosis and eradication of faults

It is important for a teacher to be able to recognise common faults in handwriting so that treatment can be given to eradicate them. The need for periodic revision has already been discussed. The first part of this chapter is concerned with the diagnosis and eradication of common faults among schoolchildren.

Faulty pencil hold

Many small children grip the pencil too tightly or incorrectly with the result that they tend to apply too much pressure and cannot produce smooth and rhythmic writing. One common faulty grip is the hold involving thumb together with first and second fingers, allowing the pencil to rest on the third. With this grip pressure is increased enormously, the pencil tends to be forced into a perpendicular position and tension prevents relaxed hand movements. A teacher can become aware of such faults by observing the children writing, but an experienced teacher is frequently able to make this diagnosis from examining a piece of writing.

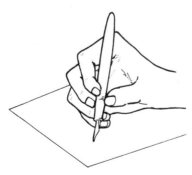

The recommended grip has already been described in Chapter 5. Extra emphasis can be given to its value by having the child write with the first finger disengaged to show how small a part it plays in gripping the pencil. Alternatively, children with this difficulty can be told to grip the pencil so lightly with the thumb and second finger that they are able to tap the pencil gently with the forefinger.

Common errors in letter formation

Children who receive good instruction during their early attempts at writing should develop good habits from the beginning. However, a teacher may find that for various reasons some pupils in the class do make fundamental mistakes which must be identified and eradicated as soon as possible. Errors commonly encountered include:

a) The enlargement of lower-case 's' to upper-case size or somewhere in between – *s*ugar, shell*S*. (Suggestions for drawing attention to the relative sizes of letters are given on page 17.)

b) The enlargement of the curved part of a lower-case 'k' – *k*

c) Mirror writing, reversals and inversions.

Mirror writing is quite rare, perhaps only one in several hundred children exhibit this phenomenon. Although the problem is more common among the mentally defective it is not a sign of mental deficiency and some outstandingly intelligent people have possessed the facility.

When mirror writing does occur it is usually in a left-handed child for whom the motor action from right to left is more natural. Most normal children can be helped to overcome the tendency by stressing the left to right direction of conventional writing but some less able children will require a clear visual indication of the correct side to start their writing. They may also be helped through carefully directed tracing activities. It is important that teachers understand the nature of the mirror-writer's problems and provide helpful support and guidance to prevent the habit continuing beyond the early stages of learning.

Children frequently read words in the reverse direction, reading 'saw' for 'was', 'tap' for 'pat', etc., and they often spell words in reverse order when writing. Similar confusion occurs in forming letters which are composed of similarly-shaped parts – for example, 'b' and 'd', 'p' and 'q', 'w' and 'm'. Children who confuse these letters require extra emphasis on writing direction and other aspects of visual discrimination. *The Pictogram System* by L. Wendon (38) is helpful in this connexion and is discussed more fully later. Materials utilising the tactile sense, such as the letter books of *Language in Action* (25), can provide an added dimension to aid the child.

Perhaps the most common of all reversals is 'b' and 'd'. Some children are helped to avoid this pitfall through the following 'bed' diagram. Discussion and reproduction of the diagram aids accurate memory recall and children experiencing this particular difficulty can be encouraged to draw the diagram as a check when in doubt. Additionally, children can be encouraged to print a capital letter 'B' and then erase the top curve.

d) The tendency to exaggerate insignificant parts of letters. For example:

q for a   h for n

This exaggeration often occurs when a child goes back to a letter to reinforce the protruding part of the letter.

e) Another source of trouble resulting from lack of instruction in the early stages is the practice of forming the letter 'O' as a clockwise circle and consequently the letter 'd' as a clockwise circle and a stick.

ð   ơ   ɗ   instead of   O a d

When this error persists into the stage of joined writing it gives rise to ᴕ instead of ʊ ; e.g. *boy* instead of *boy* .

A teacher discovering errors in children's writing will wish to devise treatment to break the bad habits formed. Possible useful techniques have been mentioned throughout this guide, and particular attention to remedies will be found in the second half of this chapter.

The left-handed child

The problems of the left-handed child were discussed in Chapter 5. But it might be helpful here to repeat initially the main points of advice.

a) Pen hold should be between thumb and second finger, but the place of grip should be further from the point than for right-handers.

b) The angle of the pen to the plane of the paper (45°) will be difficult to achieve, so specially-angled nibs for left-handers are recommended.

c) Diagonal ligatures will involve pushing instead of pulling unless the wrist is twisted. The alternative solution is the use of a smooth, rounded nib. This will obviate digging into the paper but will not allow for the production of shaded writing.

d) Paper for writing should be placed slightly to the left of a line with the centre of the body and be either parallel to the edge of the desk or, preferably, tilted to the right.

e) If possible, the source of light should be on the right side of the child.

There are two other aspects to be dealt with here. One is the importance of the teacher showing a confident attitude with regard to the left-handed child's prospects of learning to write well. Although the left-hander will require sympathy and additional guidance, we must not give the impression that a good standard cannot be achieved by a left-handed writer. Many left-handed writers achieve an extremely high standard. The other is the question of whether a left-handed beginner should be encouraged to change to the right hand. General opinion is that psychological harm is done in trying to change over a child in whom left-handed dominance is already established. Bearing in mind the programme of activities in preparation for learning to write recommended in

Chapter 2, there may be an opportunity to reorientate a very small child before left-handed dominance is fully established. A. J. Harris (16) has devised a series of tests of lateral dominance and it may be possible to ascertain through use of the appropriate parts of these tests whether a particular child could be encouraged to change without harm.

In *The Backward Child* (3), Sir Cyril Burt also puts forward a suggestion summarised below that may be helpful in this connexion. A young child who, at the beginning stages of learning to write, appears to be left-handed can be observed through the following procedure.

First invite the child to come and show you on a blackboard a pattern-drawing task he has already mastered, having ensured that the blackboard he is to write on will need to be cleaned. As he approaches, hand him a duster to clean the board. He may well take this with his left hand and start cleaning. While he is doing this offer him the chalk so that he is obliged to take it with his right hand.

The testing time is when he starts to draw. He may use his right hand which already holds the chalk, or alternatively he may feel the need to put down the duster and change the chalk over to his left hand. If his reaction is to use his right hand, he may not be a committed left-hander at all, and I think the teacher would be justified in carefully encouraging the child to use the right hand. We must always be very careful not to force a change or make a left-hander feel inadequate or guilty, but there is no doubt that the writing conventions of our society are designed for the right-hander. Therefore, wherever possible, I feel that we should help prevent the establishment of left-handed dominance in a child.

Since the problems of left-handedness give rise to so much concern, the reader might be interested to know of a very informative tape/slide presentation on the subject. 'Left-Handedness' (Short Talk No. 5) is produced by the Centre for the Teaching of Reading, School of Education, University of Reading.

The tape presentation and the slides which illustrate it are the work of Ruth Nicholls, an educational psychologist. Many aspects of the problem are knowledgeably dealt with, and teachers concerned with the problems of left-handed children will welcome the guidance and reassurance provided.

Cross laterality

Another group of children who will require a great deal of patience and understanding are those showing cross-lateral characteristics. There does not appear to be a great deal known about this condition, although some investigators estimate that over twenty per cent of children are affected to some degree.

As long ago as 1942, Schonell wrote in *Backwardness in the Basic Subjects* (31) that there were more cross-lateral children among retarded pupils than among normal ones. Most people have dominant right eyes and right hands. A smaller number have dominant left eyes and left hands and their predicaments are discussed in the preceding pages. Their handicap lies simply in the conventions of written English which favour the right-side dominants.

The cross laterals, who may be left-eye/right-hand or right-eye/left-hand dominant tend to be confused over direction of print, and their difficulties may be revealed through the continuing presence of the following symptoms:

a) reversals of letters – for example, 'p' and 'q', 'b' and 'd'

b) reversals of simple words – for example, 'on' and 'no', 'was' and 'saw'

c) incorrect letter-order in spelling

d) cramped handwriting

e) insufficient output of written expression in relation to general intelligence and oral ability

f) emotional instability.

Of course, it does not follow that every child exhibiting these tendencies is cross-lateral, nor does it follow that all cross-lateral children will be retarded, but it might be thought advisable to try to ascertain whether children experiencing these difficulties are cross-lateral, and give them individual attention and additional left-to-right practice.

Handedness may be ascertained through general observation but a test for this purpose is also described in the section on left-handedness. Many simple tests for eye dominance might be devised, but one possibility is to invite the child to view distant objects through a telescope or a cardboard tube.

Any reader acquainted with the dyslexia controversy may be struck by the similarity between the symptoms listed here for cross-laterality and those listed by writers on dyslexia. Margaret Newton of Aston University writes in her monograph, *Dyslexia: a Guide to Teaching* (27), of the difficulties caused by unstable perceptual patterns which arise when there is ambilateral function in place of dominance. She explains how these difficulties prevent the consistent learning of order and direction – visually, auditorily and graphically.

In connexion with her work on the Aston Index, which is designed to indicate those children who are likely to be at risk in achieving literacy, Margaret Newton has collaborated with June Eaves to produce some notes on the problems of the left-handed child in relation to a left/right changeover:

It frequently happens that teachers and parents are faced with the problem of a left-handed child starting school in a 'right-handed' world. Because the written forms of language scan from left to right in English-speaking (and many other) countries, it would seem that the left-handed child is at a disadvantage in acquiring this one-directional skill. He will have a motor tendency in the first place to write from right to left of the page. Then when writing in the *required* direction, a left-handed child will be obscuring his line of text as he writes, thus depriving him of some continuity of experience.

There will also be conflicts of direction, both perceptual and motor and a tendency to regress therefore, or make non-fluent movements, or inconsistencies in the slope of writing. Sometimes a left-handed child is also left-eyed and will be visually scanning the material from right to left. Consequently spelling patterns become disturbed as well as the arrangement of words in a sentence; in fact he will have difficulties with a fluency of reading and writing in general. Because of these ambiguities in direction, work is slowed down and undue time has to be taken to complete the ordinary demands of prose writing.

What advice could be given therefore to help a child with these left-sided tendencies in a right-sided world?

It is very difficult to generalise about modifying the left/right motor/directional biases of each individual child as each one has a different underlying constellation of laterality ('sidedness'). I think one must observe very closely the *total* behaviour of the child as he uses hand, eye and foot for all the activities of the day. If the left hand is used continually for all the finer movements of writing, cutting (scissors), painting, spoon, knife, etc., it would appear that there is a strong organisational (internal) preference for 'leftness' in motor tasks. In this case one would not change to right-handed mode. If, however, the child used either hand at random both for fine and gross movements and was having severe directional problems in writing and reading, a programme of remedial help could be devised starting from a physiological level, which could mean emphasising *right*-handed motor activity in a left/right direction. These children seem to be rare however amongst the total population of ambilateral people (many of whom, although able to use both hands and both eyes, in the final analysis prefer one side or the other for motor movements).

Because handedness is a part of an underlying complex organisation in the brain, the advice seems to be, in the main, not to change a child except in the rare circumstances mentioned above (especially over the age of 5) but to give him strategies within his own patterning for dealing with the demands of school learning, etc. These would include of course many left-to-right-type patternings, tracings, always starting from a brightly coloured margin on the left – helping the child to notice differences in direction, especially in letters, words, sentences, etc., using a book marker, both for drawing along the line as one reads, and also for moving down the page on the left indicating the beginning of each line of text. It is a continual process of over-teaching, over-learning, to enable the child to adapt to the desired directional/sequential system when he himself would perhaps acquire more easily a spatial or iconic one. One can reinforce directional awareness in other activities, e.g., arrangement of tools, pencils, play equipment, table placings and everyday objects of life.

Needless to say, one gives the child many opportunities to achieve in his own skills of painting, modelling, kit-making, etc., to achieve satisfactory psychological development, as well as specific language-orientated creative writing, spelling pattern learning and 'reading for fun'.

For more detailed applications to spelling and writing, we recommend to you *Diagnosis in the Classroom* by Gill Cotterell, published by the Centre for the Teaching of Reading, School of Education, University of Reading.

Handwriting and dyslexia

A consideration of the reasons behind the poor writing which is so often a feature of the dyslexic's work is presented in *The Problem of Handwriting* by E. Waller (37).

Examples are provided of dyslexic children's writing and a variety of underlying problems are discussed. Useful approaches and techniques for improvement are recommended together with the following apparatus:

a) *Frostig Visual Perception Programme*, N.F.E.R. Publishing Co., 2 Jennings Buildings, Thames Avenue, Windsor, Berks SL4 1QS.

b) *Edith Norrie Letter-Case* (English Version), Helen Arkell Dyslexia Centre, 14 Crondace Road, London SW6 4BB.

c) *Tutorpack Teaching Machine*, Helen Arkell Dyslexia Centre.

Line of direction

A few children persist in writing in lines which rise or fall towards the end. This tendency can often be eradicated by reminders about posture, the positioning of the writing paper and encouragement to write parallel with the edge of the paper. Should these measures fail, then the use of lines will have to be resorted to. For a beginner it is helpful if the teacher rules lines at a width appropriate to the child's natural writing size. For an older child, who wants the freedom of layout provided by plain paper, guidelines can be provided to fit under the writing paper. These can either be made by the teacher with Indian ink on thin card, or manufactured guideline cards may be obtained from A. Brown & Sons Ltd, Hull, and from Platignum Ltd.

Relationship of ascenders and descenders to the line of writing

For those children who have difficulty in comprehending the way in which the writing space is divided into three, practice frames can be provided consisting of three equal squares placed vertically as illustrated in Chapter 3. Sheets of paper with guidelines similar in appearance to music staves can be duplicated to provide practice in achieving correct relationships to the writing flow. In this connexion display charts and sets of individual letter cards ruled to emphasise the relationships are useful. The same devices can be employed to illustrate the relative proportions of letters.

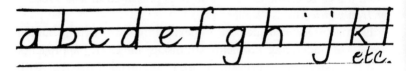

Techniques and materials for dealing with the problems of slow learners

Perceptual Training Pack

This pack was devised by A. E. Tansley and G. Davies (and published by E. J. Arnold) and has been tried and tested for ten years. The pack consists of cards, shapes and a workbook which provide a programme of activities to aid the development of pre-reading and pre-writing skills. These materials should be very helpful for children with learning disabilities in the areas of:

a) motor control
b) hand–eye co-ordination
c) perception of form and spatial relationships.

Learning Development Aids

The first range of aids produced under this title by a publishing company of the same name, consists of twelve sets of cards. Topics covered include spatial relationships, classification, sequencing, shape, pattern and visual recall. Use of these materials by children with learning difficulties should lead to improvement in several areas of learning associated with pre-reading and pre-writing.

The Pictogram System

A system of picture associations for letters, together with a 'Letter Land' mythology has been developed by Lyn Wendon. Her teaching materials are published under the name *The Pictogram System* (38).

The use of pictograms is especially recommended for slow learners because it allows the teacher's verbal instructions for letter formation to become concrete and specific. Children's interest and memory recall are increased by the characterisation of the letters, and instructions to aid correct formation are both clear and imaginative. The following examples serve to illustrate the principles involved.

For both capital and small letter shapes the teacher is in a position to give verbal instructions by referring to the picture version of the plain letter. For example, the instructions for forming 'd' and 'h', as quoted from the SET I Teacher's Manual, are as follows.

To write this letter:
Always start to write this letter by stroking Dicky Duck on the back, smoothing his feathers down towards his tail. (Dicky Duck loves having his feathers stroked.) Then bring your pencil down under his body and all the way up to the top of his neck.

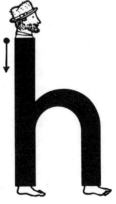

To write this letter:
Draw a straight line from the top of the Hairy Hat Man's shoulder, right down his back and his first leg. Then draw the hump of his second leg.

The Pictogram System is far more than just an aid to correct letter formation. It has been fully developed so that phonic rules may be dramatised and explained through the pictures which represent the letters. Its mythology includes stories to illuminate the perplexing irregularities and contradictions of English spelling. However, I have referred to the materials in this guide because of their value to children experiencing difficulty in learning to form the letters. Even teachers who do not wish to introduce the Pictogram mythology to their children may find a study of the materials and teacher's manuals very enlightening and helpful to their own understanding of the processes involved in letter formation.

Teaching strategies for helping children with severe writing problems

The following suggestions for dealing with severe writing problems are intended for guidance in a one-to-one situation and will probably need to be sustained patiently over a considerable period of time.

Having isolated an error through observing the child write, a teacher can commence a teaching programme designed gradually to eradicate it. The child is asked to copy a word containing the troublesome letter.

Stage 1. Before the child attempts to make the letter the teacher presents a correct model and gives very clear instruction on how to make the letter. The teacher then watches the child's performance and praises success.

Stage 2. After several such sessions at regular intervals, when it is felt the child is able to remember what is involved, though performance may still be uneven, the teacher puts the responsibility on the child by asking, 'What do you have to remember when you write this word?' The word includes the letter which has been the subject of the lesson. This approach leads the child to watch for the difficulties he recognises and helps build his confidence to overcome them. The child then writes the word and the teacher praises his performance particularly over the key letter.

Stage 3. The child is left to write a word containing the problem letter without any prior discussion. The teacher then evaluates, praising success and asking the child to re-examine if there is an error and to correct it.

It must be stressed again that this kind of teaching strategy is only possible in a one-to-one situation, and is only recommended for use with children experiencing grave difficulty in learning to write.

The tactile sense

A child with severe visual and motor difficulties may be helped enormously through the tactile sense.

a) Some children are helped if the teacher makes the letter with a finger on the palm of the child's hand.

b) Letters can be cut from sandpaper, felt, hessian or other rough material for the child to trace with the tip of the finger. Similarly letters can be made by use of a glue-pen and sprinkling sand. These tactile letters should be mounted on card so that directional arrows can be drawn and the teacher will need to direct the child's finger as the letter shape is followed (see also the Letter Books of *Language in Action* (25)).

c) The preparation of duplicated sheets on which letters are formed by a series of dots can be most useful, especially if directional arrows are provided to guide the correct completion of the letters.

Teaching machines

One of the problems when faced with a child with severe difficulties in learning to write is finding sufficient time to spend with the child. As has been stressed throughout this guide, it is useless to provide a model of handwriting without adequate advice and instruction. For a child who needs a great deal of attention in this matter it is worth exploring the use of teaching machines.

TAPE RECORDERS COMBINED WITH PREPARED TEACHING MATERIALS
If a child with great difficulty in learning to write can be given specific worksheets for tracing, copying, etc., and if the teacher records appropriate instruction on to a cassette tape, it is possible for the child to have repeated practice on his own as frequently as necessary. There are advantages in that it is possible to prepare

material for a specific purpose for a particular child. It is a time-consuming operation, but the time utilised is not the vital in-school hours when personal contact with all the children in the class is so important. The main problem hindering independent operation by children is the difficulty of running the cassette back to the right spot for a re-run.

SYNCROFAX

This more sophisticated machine allows the preparation of specially-designed remedial worksheets for poor writers and has the advantage of overcoming the difficulty of finding the starting point on the cassette tape. In essence, a Syncrofax Teaching Machine consists of a platform on which a special sheet rests together with a built-in recording and playback system. One side of a Syncrofax sheet provides a plain surface on which model letter shapes or skeleton letters for copying or tracing can be drawn. The reverse side is specially treated to allow the recording of up to four minutes of speech. It is therefore possible to provide practice work illustrated with directional arrows, etc., and accompanied by spoken instructions which guide the children as they trace, complete or reproduce the work.

With this system it is possible to prepare material to remedy specific faults for particular children but it is also possible to build up a collection of sheets dealing with fairly common faults, so that they can be readily available.

One practical tip. It is wise to use a cassette tape-recorder when working out how to pace the teaching commentary for each sheet.

FROM LEFT TO WRITE

Another interesting and useful scheme for helping slow learners master the techniques of writing and reading is *From Left to Write* (22). This has a programmed learning approach, and is published by Autobates Learning Systems. It is available in roll form for use with Autobates Teaching Machines or in book form for use with chinagraph pencils on an acetate shield.

The programmes are intended for young infants, slow learners and ESN pupils. I feel that the greatest benefit will be with older slow learners, but agree that Book 1 would possibly be helpful as a basis for discussion with infants with weak visual discrimination.

There are ten programmes available in roll or book form together with a teacher's handbook and four expendable workbooks. Thorough attention is paid to the left-to-right convention of written English as well as to correct letter-formation and the introduction of a basic writing and reading vocabulary.

Books 1 and 2 are devoted to improving visual discrimination and teaching correct formation of letters and numerals. A colour code involving three colours, starting and finishing stars and directional arrows is introduced to aid correct formation. Learning experiences are introduced at a controlled rate and provision is made for instant verification that the child's response is correct.

Programmes 3a to 6b (eight in all) present about sixty thoughtfully selected words so that practice in letter formation occurs in meaningful contexts while the child's efforts continue to be encouraged and supported through the use of colour coding. These words are introduced gradually with seven frames devoted to each word as illustrated below.

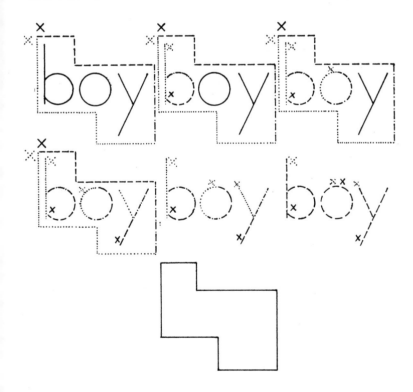

The learning of these sixty words is further reinforced in many ways through work in the workbooks.

The overhead projector

The overhead projector is not always fully appreciated as a teaching tool. As an aid for teaching handwriting, particularly to older children with learning difficulties, it has much to commend it.

Its use permits the teacher to face a group, and so observe their accuracy and rate of progress. It is also conducive to the good relationships which are important for remedial work. The pupils are able to see the teacher's pen at work and to see the direction and sequence of movements involved in forming letters. Then, when the children are reproducing the models of letter shapes on the screen, the teacher is free to move among the group giving individual attention. The teacher is also able to use prepared transparencies made at a convenient time.

In *The New Media Challenge* (36), another of the Language Guides, N. E. Trowbridge warns of the difficulty in writing on a switched-on, overhead projector and stresses the need for preliminary practice. He also gives many useful hints for efficient use of the machine.

Further Reading

Burt, Sir Cyril (3)
Suggestions for helping left-handed children are offered, and the advisability of effecting a changeover from left hand to right hand is discussed (pages 337–40).

Clark, M. M. (4)
A report on an investigation into the problems of left-handed children in Scotland.

Fagg, R. (7)
Advice for the left-handed writer will be found on page 21.

Fairbanks, A. (8)
Advice for helping the left-handed child is given (page 100).

Gourdie, T. (11)
Advice for the left-handed writer is provided (page 58).

Guilliford, R. (15)
On pages 73–6 a plea is made for more attention to the problems of poor writers and advice for helping the left-handed writer, in particular, is offered.

Harris, A. J. (16)
Harris Tests of Lateral Dominance is available from the National Foundation for Educational Research in England and Wales for use by clinical psychologists and other persons with specific training.

Presland, J. (29)
In this article, an educational psychologist analyses the learning activities needed for the successful achievement of handwriting. Utilising psychological knowledge and theory about the learning process he discusses the range of problems and recommends approaches, techniques and materials.

Grant, R. (44)
A 32 page booklet of exercises to develop motor control and sequential writing which would be of particular value to secondary school children with problems in this area.

Final word

There is no doubt that learning to write is a complex skill and most children will require systematic instruction if they are to achieve a pleasant, legible, fluent style of handwriting. They need to practise the basic hand movements and patterns appropriate to their stages of development. When they use the skill for its true purpose of communication they should be encouraged to achieve a good standard of handwriting but not at the expense of content. If the climate of teacher-pupil relationship is right there will be a healthy attitude to the whole question of standards.

In most skills-learning it is true to say that faults acquired in the early stages are difficult to eradicate. This is certainly true of the skill of handwriting and teachers of young infants must consider their role very carefully indeed. A chapter on the diagnosis and eradication of faults has been included to help teachers with children whose difficulties in learning to write persist into junior and secondary schools. The reader is reminded that children causing grave concern in this direction should also be referred to the educational psychologist and/or the school doctor for expert diagnosis.

Essential to the realisation of the aims discussed in this guide is the skill and expertise of the teacher. In the writer's view, there must be a whole school programme, preferably decided on through discussion among the staff. The head teacher has a responsibility to instigate and lead such discussions, and to ensure that the experience of colleagues with special expertise is utilised. In this way a coherent school programme, acceptable to those required to teach it, should be achieved and put in writing as a guide.

There is an obvious need to include consideration of the techniques of teaching handwriting in initial teacher-training courses for all teachers. The subject must also be included in the increasing provision of in-service training. Teachers would then have the knowledge of basic principles and alternative styles on which to base decisions when compiling the school guide. Once the decision as to style or combinations of styles has been made, teachers should increase their own efficiency through practice and experiment. Awareness of the children's problems in acquiring the style develops through close observation as they work.

My recommended programme for the teaching of handwriting – that is, print-script, followed by Marion Richardson and finally a modified form of Italic – is likely to be controversial. However, it is not claimed that this is the only way. The suggestion is simply offered because it has been found to work, and as an example of the type of programme that might be devised by a school staff. It is hoped that the information and ideas presented in this guide will aid other teachers in deciding what is, for them, the best approach to this complex but essential task of teaching the skills of handwriting.

Aids for teaching handwriting

*E. J. Arnold Teaching Aids
a) Synchrofax Audio Page Player (AV 072)
b) The Audio Page Recorder and Playback Machine (AV 071)
c) Audio distribution centre and headphones (AV 039)
d) Audio page software including Phonic Alphabet Programme
e) Perceptual Training Pack.

*ESA Teaching Aids
Basic Motor Skills Booklets 1–8.

*From Left to Write by C. H. Jones (Autobates, 1968)
A learning programme in the Pursuit Series.

*Learning Development Aids
Twelve sets of cards for children with learning difficulty including
a set (reference 7) which deals with visual recall.

Learning to Write by I. and R. Heaps (W. & R. Chambers)
A set of four books and tracing pads designed to make practice
fun. A graded programme starting with straight lines and progressing to the full print-script alphabet.

*'Left-Handedness' by Ruth Nicholls (Centre for Reading,
    Reading University)
A tape-slide talk on the problems and remedies for left-handed
writers.

*'Left-Right Rhyme Card' by D. H. Stott (Holmes McDougall,
    1964)

Philip and Tacey Teaching Aids
a) Pencil Control Tracing Cards and Wallet (A 113–1, 2, 3)
b) Pencil Control Wax Pencils (153–003–001–7)
c) Precept Shadow Letter Chalk-Work Tracing Sheets (R72)
d) Matrix Script Letter Tracing Stencils (R 159–1)
e) Matrix Script Letter Guide Cards (R 159–2)
f) First Steps Script Writing Books (R 142–1)
g) Second Steps Script Writing Books (R 142–2)
h) Useful Words to Spell and Write Books (R 172).

The Pictogram System by Lyn Wendon (Pictogram Supplies, 1972)
A multi-sensory approach to reading and writing.

Platignum Teaching Aids
a) A set of four copybooks: 1. Firsthand Writing; 2. Cursive; 3. Round Style; 4. Italic
b) A set of three wall-charts: 1. Cursive; 2. Round Style; 3. Italic
c) A set of instruction leaflets: 1. Cursive; 2. Round Style; 3. Italic
d) Line-guide sheets made of plastic for use when writing on plain paper
e) A wide range of writing instruments.

Osmiroid Teaching Aids
a) A set of three wall-charts: 1. Cursive; 2. Italic; 3. Marion Richardson.
b) A set of five leaflets: 1. Cursive; 2. Italic; 3. Marion Richardson; 4. Left-handed writing styles; 5. Play with a pen
c) An Italic handwriting guide booklet
d) A film 'How to Write Well' available to schools (free on loan).
e) Pens and range of nibs.

For details of teaching materials for specific styles of joined handwriting see Chapter 5.

* Recommended for use with remedial children.

Addresses

E. J. Arnold & Son Ltd, Butterley Street, Leeds, LS10 1AX.

Autobates Learning Systems Ltd, Whitestone House, Lutterworth Road, Nuneaton, Warwickshire.

The Centre for the Teaching of Reading, University of Reading, 29 Eastern Avenue, Reading, Berks.

W. & R. Chambers Ltd, 11 Thistle Street, Edinburgh 2.

K. Drummond, (Bookseller specialising in Calligraphy), 30 Hart Grove, Ealing Common, London W5 3NB.

E.S.A. Ltd, Pinnacles, P.O. Box 22, Harlow, Essex EM19 5AY.

The Helen Arkell Dyslexia Centre, 14 Crondace Road, London SW6 4BB.

Learning Development Aids, Park Works, Norwich Road, Wisbech, Cambs. PE13 2AX.

Osmiroid Handwriting Service, Gosport, Hampshire.

NFER Publishing Co., 2 Jennings Buildings, Thames Avenue, Windsor, Berks. SL4 1QS.

Philip & Tacey Ltd, North Way, Andover, Hampshire SP10 5BA.

Pictogram Supplies, Barton, Cambridge CB3 7AY.

Platignum Schools Division, Six Hills Way, Stevenage, Herts. SG1 2AY.

The Society for Italic Handwriting, Secretary, Mrs Thea Mutter, 59a Arlington Road, London, NW1.

Bibliography

1 Blackie, J. *Changing the Primary School: an Integrated Approach* (Macmillan Education 1974)
2 Brennan, W., *et al.* *Look,* the Teacher's Handbook (Macmillan Education 1974)
3 Burt, Sir C. *The Backward Child* (University of London Press 1937)
4 Clark, M. M. *Teaching Left-handed Children* (ULP 1959; 2nd edn 1974)
5 Department of Education and Science. *Education: a Framework for Expansion* (HMSO 1972). White Paper
6 Department of Education and Science. *Teacher Education and Training* (HMSO 1972). The James Report
7 Fagg, R. *Everyday Writing,* Teacher's Book (ULP 1963)
8 Fairbanks, A. *The Story of Handwriting* (Faber 1970)
9 Fletcher, D., Bakewell, R. and Robertson, N. K. *Quick and Legible Handwriting,* Teacher's Manual (Oliver & Boyd 1958)
10 Giglioli, P. P. (Ed.). *Language and Social Context* (Penguin 1972)
11 Gourdie, T. *A Guide to Better Handwriting* (Studio Vista 1967)
12 Gourdie, T. *The Simple Modern Hand,* Teacher's Book (Collins 1966)
13 Gourdie, T. *I Can Write* (Macmillan Education 1974)
14 Gray, W. S. *The Teaching of Reading and Writing* (Unesco and Evans 1956)
15 Gulliford, R. *Backwardness and Educational Failure* (National Foundation for Educational Research in England and Wales 1969)

16 Harris, A. J. *Harris Tests of Lateral Dominance* (The Psychiatric Corporation, New York, 3rd edn 1958). Available from NFER

17 Haskell, S. and Paull, M. *Handbook for Basic Cognitive Skills/ Basic Motor Skills* (ESA 1974)

18 Hughes, F. *Reading and Writing Before School* (Cape 1971)

19 Inglis, A. and Gibson, E. *The Teaching of Handwriting*, Teacher's Manual to Infant Scheme (Nelson 1962). Series now called Nelson Handwriting.

20 Inglis, A. and Gibson, E. *The Teaching of Handwriting*, Teacher's Manual to Primary Scheme (Nelson 1962). Series now called Nelson Handwriting

21 Jarman, C. 'Is children's handwriting neglected?' *Where*, ACE Journal (January 1973), pp. 5–8

22 Jones, C. H. *From Left to Write*, Teacher's Handbook (Autobates 1968)

23 Mackay, D., Thompson B. and Schaub, P. *Breakthrough to Literacy*, Teacher's Manual (Longman 1970)

24 Marshall, S. *Creative Writing*, The Language Project (Macmillan Education 1974)

25 Morris, J. M., *et al. Language in Action*, The Language Project (Macmillan Education 1974)

26 Moyle, D. *The Teaching of Reading* (Ward Lock Educational 1971)

27 Newton, M. and Thomson, M. *Dyslexia: a Guide to Teaching* (University of Aston 1974)

28 Obrist, C. and Pickard, P. *Time for Reading*, Teacher's Manual (Ginn 1967)

29 Presland, J. 'Applied psychology and backwardness in handwriting' Supplement to the Association of Educational Psychology Journal Vol. II, No. 7, October 1970

30 Richardson, M. *Writing and Writing Patterns*, Teacher's Book (ULP 1935)

31 Schonell, F. J. *Backwardness in the Basic Subjects* (Oliver & Boyd 1942)

32 Stern, C. and Gould, T. S. *Children Discover Reading* (Harrap 1966)

33 Stone, C. *Beacon Writing*, Teacher's Book for Books 1 and 2 (Ginn 1957). Beacon Writing Series, Ed. A. Fairbank

34 Taylor, J. *Reading and Writing in the First School* (Allen & Unwin 1973)

35 Thomson, G. L. *The Scottish Educational Journal* (4 June 1954)

36 Trowbridge, N. E. *The New Media Challenge,* The Language Project (Macmillan Education 1974)

37 Waller, E. *The Problem of Handwriting* (Helen Arkell Dyslexia Centre 1974)

38 Wendon, L., *The Pictogram System,* Teacher's Manuals to Sets 1 and 2 (Pictogram Supplies 1973)

39 Whanslaw, H. W. *Paper Reeds and Iron Pens* (Religious Education Press 1957)

40 Yardley, A. *Exploration and Language* (Evans 1970)

41 Thomson, G. L. *The New Better Handwriting* (Carongate Publishing Ltd 1977)

42 Phillips, R. C. *The Skills of Handwriting* (R. C. Phillips Ltd Oxford 1976)

43 Smith, P. and Williams, J. *Writemaster Books 1–6* (Holmes McDougall 1979)

44 Grant, R. *Writing Exercises to Encourage Ocular Control* (Available from Mr. Grant at 21 Crescente Walk, Bognor Regis, West Sussex. 1978)

45 Young, J. and Young, P. *Write and Spell* (Oliver & Boyd 1978)

The examples which follow illustrate progression in the development of handwriting through Print-Script and the Marion Richardson style. They have been selected in accordance with the view that, although the skill of handwriting must be methodically taught, priority should be given to the purposes of writing.

One day I said to my
mum, is it Easter yet? yes
She said, and I said, good, I like
Easter. It is Fun at Easter
because my brothers are
going away camping
and I may go to see my
Antie and uncle at polegate. I
get three trains and I go over
the railway track to get
there. I love going there
because they have a cat,
a dog, a goldfish, a rabbit, and a
tortose. I feed the rabbit with
dandelins. I can go to the seaslde
from there too, so I have a
happy time.

Print-Script. Uncorrected news by a girl aged 6.

Daffadowndilly.

She wore her yellow sun – bonnet,
She wore her greenest gown,
She turned to the south wind
And curtsied up and down.
She turned to the sunlight
And shook her yellow head,
And whispered to her neighbour,
"Winter is dead."

A. A. Milne.

Marion Richardson. A poem copied for display by a boy aged 8½.

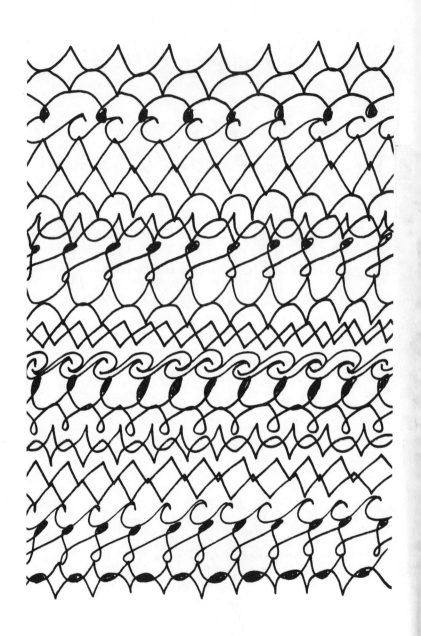

Marion Richardson. Panel of pattern.

An Invitation.

The teachers and children of the 2nd. Year cordially invite Mr. Smith to attend their Maritime Exhibition in their corridor, at his convenience.

Marion Richardson. An invitation written by a boy aged 8.

Explorers.

The furry moth explores the night,
The fish discover cities drowned,
And moles and worms and ants explore
The many cupboards underground.

The soaring lark explores the sky,
And gulls explore the stormy seas;
The busy squirrel rummages
Among the attics of the trees.

James Reeves.

Marion Richardson. A poem copied for display by a girl aged 10½.

A SEA DIRGE

Full fathom five thy
      father lies:
Of his bones are
      coral made;
Those are pearls that
      were his eyes:
Nothing of him that
      doth fade,
But doth suffer a
      sea change
Into something rich
      and strange.

Marion Richardson. An example written at speed by the author.

Index

aesthetics *xii*, *27*, *44*, *51*, *53*, *56*, *57*
Ahiram King *2*
alternative styles *viii*, *26–38*, *53*, *54*, *58*, *76*
anthologies *57*
anti-clockwise *19*, *61*
ascenders *4*, *18*, *19*, *20*, *22*, *27*, *41*, *42*, *43*, *50*, *67*
Atkinson, Delia *37*
Autobates Teaching Machine *72*

Babylonians *1*
Bakewell, R. *36*
ball and stick *13*, *61*
ball-point pens *46*
Basic Motor Skills Booklets *8*, *11*
Beacon Writing *28*, *36*
Blackie, J. *xiii*
boustrophedon *3*
Brahma *1*
Breakthrough to Literacy *14*, *18*, *19*
Brennan, W. *11*
Bullock Report *vii*, *viii*
burin *4*
Burt, Cyril *63*, *74*
Byblos *2*

capitals *3*, *13*, *14*, *16*, *23*, *24*, *44*, *50*, *58*
cave paintings *1*
changing left to right *62*, *66*, *74*
changing style *39*, *52*, *53*, *58*
Chinese *1*
civil service style *27*
Clark, Margaret *48*, *51*, *74*
classroom organisation *xi*, *xiii*, *6*, *13*, *18*, *21*, *31*
clockwise *19*, *61*
copper-plate *4*, *27*, *44*
copybooks and cards *20*, *31*, *36*, *37*, *44*, *45*, *53*, *58*
copy writing *16*, *19*, *57*
Cotterell, Gill *66*
creative writing *vii*, *xii*, *xiii*, *53*, *54*, *56*, *64*, *66*
cross-laterality *64*, *65*, *68*
cuneiform *2*
cursive *2*, *3*, *12*, *26*, *27*, *35*, *44*
decoration *40*, *56*, *57*, *58*

demotic style *2*
descenders *4*, *18*, *19*, *20*, *22*, *27*, *44*, *50*, *67*
descriptive terminology *19*
diagnosis of faults *45*, *59*, *60–6*
display *xii*, *18*, *45*, *51*, *53*, *56*, *57*, *58*
dominance *47*, *62–6*
drafts *53*, *57*, *58*
Dryad aids *37*
duplicated worksheets *21*, *67*, *71*
dyslexia *64*, *65*, *67*

Edith Norrie Letter Case *67*
Education: A framework for expansion *x*
Egyptians *1*
elliptical letter shapes *12*, *28*, *35*, *52*, *58*
emotional problems *64*
engraving *4*
eradication of faults *viii*, *59–75*
Everyday Writing *19*, *27*, *33*, *34*, *37*

Fagg, Ruth *19*, *37*, *51*, *74*
Fairbank, Alfred *1*, *5*, *36*, *74*
fair copies *53*, *57*, *58*
families of letters *20*, *54*, *55*
faults *45*, *46*, *47*, *48*, *54*, *59*, *62*, *67*, *75*, *76*
faulty grip *46*, *47*, *48*, *59*, *60*
film-loops and strips *37*
Firsthand Writing *20*, *27*, *33*, *34*, *37*
Fletcher, D. *36*
fluency *35*, *40*, *65*
formation of letters *xii*, *xiii*, *13–19*, *20–25*, *35*, *46*, *60*, *61*, *68–70*
fountain pens *46*
From Left to Right programme *72*
Frostig Visual Perception Pack *67*

Gibson, E. *36*, *51*, *58*
Gould, T. S. *11*
Gourdie, Tom *5*, *25*, *30*, *31*, *36*, *37*, *38*, *51*, *74*
Gray, William S. *12*, *25*
Greeks *1*
Guide to Better Handwriting *31*
Gulliford, R. *75*

half-uncials *3*
handedness *62–6*
Harris, A. J. *63, 75*
Haskell, Simon *8, 11*
Hermes *1*
hieratic style *2*
hieroglyphic style *2*
Hindus *1*
Horsburgh, D. *36*
Hughes, F. *25*

I can write style *30, 31, 37*
ideograms *2*
Inglis, A. *36, . ., 58*
initial teacher training *x, 76*
in-service training *x, 76*
integrated day *21, 31*
inversion *60, 61*
Isis *1*
italic *viii, 4, 26, 28, 29, 30, 31, 35, 36,
    52, 58, 76*

James Report *x, xiii*
Jarman, C. *xiii*
joined-script *26, 27, 35, 40*

Lancaster, Joseph *4*
language experience *17, 18*
Language in Action *10, 18, 61, 71*
lateral dominance *63, 65*
layout *19, 44, 56, 57, 58, 67*
Learning Development Aids *10, 68*
left-handed children *47–50, 60–6, 74,
    75*
left-right change *62–6, 74*
left-right direction *18, 60, 64–6*
legibility *53*
letter families *20, 54, 55*
letter formation *xii, xiii, 13–19, 20–5,
    35, 46, 60, 61, 68–70*
letter templates *67, 71*
letter writing *57*
ligatures *40–5, 49, 56, 62*
light *50, 62*
lined and unlined paper *23, 50, 51, 67*
Look *11*
looped style *4, 27, 44*
lower-case *3, 13, 14, 16*

Mackay, D. *25*
magazine *57*
margins *56, 57*
Marshall, Sybil *xiii, 58*
memory recall *6, 10*
middle school years *52, 58*
mirror writing *60*
Morris, Joyce M. *11, 25*
motivation *6, 17, 19, 27, 52*
motor development *6, 8, 12, 15, 17,
    35, 45, 52, 64–6, 68*
Moyle, D. *xiv, 71*

Nebo *1*
Newton, Margaret *65*
nib *3, 4, 28, 46, 48, 49, 62*
Niccole, Niccoli *4*
Nicholls, Ruth *63*

Obrist, C. *11*
orientation *9*
Osmiroid aids *30, 36, 37*
overhead projector *74*

parchment *3*
papyrus *2*
parents *13–16, 21, 27*
patterns *7, 8, 15, 19, 28, 31, 32, 35, 40,
    46, 54, 55, 56, 57, 58, 68, 76*
Paul, Margaret *8, 11*
pen *3, 4, 26, 46, 48*
pen angle *47–9, 62*
pen/pencil grip *31, 46, 47, 48, 59, 60,
    62*
penna *3*
Perceptual Training Pack *68*
personal style *28, 35, 54, 58, 76*
Phoenician *2*
Pickard, P. *11*
pictograms *1, 2*
Pictogram System *61, 68, 69*
placing of paper *31, 48, 49, 62, 67*
Platignum aids *20, 27, 29, 33, 34, 36,
    37*
policy chool *vii, xi, 26, 35, 39, 52, 58,
    76*
posture *25, 46, 49, 67*
Presland, J. *75*

printing-press *4*
print-script *viii*, *12*, *13*, *15–18*, *25*, *33*,
    35, *39*, *76*
programmed learning *72*
proportions of letters *17*, *18*, *22*, *44*,
    50, *60*, *67*

Quick and Legible Handwriting *36*
quill *3*, *4*

readiness *6*, *7*, *15*, *17*
reed pen *2*
remedial *11*, *21*, *22*
Renaissance Italic Handwriting Books
    36
reversal *60*, *61*, *64*
revision *52–4*, *56*, *58*, *59*
Richardson, Marion *viii*, *8*, *11*, *26*, *32*,
    33, *35*, *37*, *40*, *41*, *42*, *43*, *44*, *51*, *52*,
    56, *58*, *76*
Robertson, N. K. *36*
Roman *3*
Round style *27*, *33*, *34*, *37*

Schonell, Fred *64*
school policy *vii*, *xi*, *26*, *35*, *39*, *52*, *58*,
    76
Semitic *2*
Simple Modern Hand *31*, *36*, *37*
size of writing *19*, *44*, *50*, *51*
slope/slant *12*, *58*
slow-learners *11*, *21*, *22*, *52*, *61–75*
Society for Italic Handwriting *28*
spacing *18*, *19*, *20*, *44*, *51*
standards *xii*, *20*, *44*, *45*, *52–7*, *62*, *76*
Stern, C. *11*
Stone, C. *51*
strategy for individual help *70*
stylus *2*
Sumerians *1*

syncrofax *72*

tactile sense *18*, *22*, *61*, *71*
Tansley, A. E. *68*
tape recorders *71*
Tape/Slide presentation Left-
    handedness *63*
Taylor, J. *xiv*
teacher-pupil relationships *ix*, *xi*, *20*,
    45, *54*, *62*, *70*, *74*, *76*
teaching machines *72*
Teaching of Handwriting (Nelson) *28*,
    36
teaching techniques *viii*, *ix*, *xi* *13*, *17–*
    21, *31*, *39–45*, *51*, *53*, *54*, *61–75*
Tests of lateral dominance *63*, *75*
thicks and thins *3*, *28*
Thomson, George L. *31*
Thoth *1*
Time for Reading *8*
tracing *7*, *22*, *37*, *60*, *66*, *71*
Trowbridge, N. E. *74*
Ts'ang Chieh *1*
Tutor pack Teaching Machine *67*

Vere Foster *36*
visual perception *6*, *9*, *10*, *17*, *45*, *65*,
    68, *71*
visual recall cards *68*

Waller *67*
Wendon, Lyn *61*
Whanslaw, H. W. *5*
woodblock *4*
Worthy, W. *36*
Writing and Writing Patterns *8*, *37*
writing guide line cards *67*
writing size *19*, *44*, *50*, *51*
writing tools *2*, *3*, *4*, *7*, *15*, *25*, *45*, *46*

Yardley, A. *xiv*